PHIL TU...
A TO Z OF CRICKET

SPORTSBOOKS

Phil Tufnell's AtoZ of Cricket

© Phil Tufnell 2003

Photographs supplied by Action Images (except where credited)
Cover image taken by Richard Heathcote

Cover design: Kath Northam

A CIP catalogue record for this book is available from the British Library

ISBN 1899807 17 9

Printed by and bound by Creative Print & Design, Wales.

Published by SportsBooks Ltd
PO Box 422
Cheltenham
GL50 2YN
United Kingdom
Tel: 08700 713 965
Fax: 08700 750 888
email   randall@sportsbooks.ltd.uk
Website   www.sportsbooks.ltd.uk

FOREWORD

When I started thinking about jotting down a few of the things that had actually remained lodged in my head after nearly 20 years as a pro I had just seen my bowling spanked all over The Oval by the Aussies. It was about 90 degrees in the shade, our mates from down under had racked up 641 and we were on our way to an innings defeat. No change there then, but what I didn't realise was that would be that on the Test playing front.

I had an inkling that I wasn't in the front of the England selectors' minds when I wasn't picked for the winter tour but I was ready to roll my arm over in the county game for a few more years.

Two years on and things have certainly changed a bit. I've managed to go from bowling a bit of left arm spin to shoving grubs down my throat in the outback and scrabbling around for firewood. Not exactly what they teach you in the indoor school at Lord's. Being in 'I'm a Celebrity, Get Me Out of Here' was all a bit of a laugh, but I'm a cricketer (or ex-cricketer) really and have had the time of my life playing, and being paid to play, the game in some of the best places in the world.

The era in which I started playing Test cricket was dominated by the Bothams, Gowers and Gattings and I was a lucky boy to be surrounded by legends like them when I got into the England side.

After that little lot I had the privilege to play with people like Athers, Big Gus Fraser and little Thorpey and the misfortune to see my bowling hit into the stands of some of the world's most picturesque grounds by the likes of Brian Lara, Sachin Tendulkar and Steve Waugh. Cheers boys.

Luckily I've managed to remember a few of the things that happened and got them down on paper. The blokes I've played with, the places I've been and − in my new position as a cricket analyst − a bit of technical waffle. Here is my AtoZ of cricket. Enjoy.

Phil Tufnell

Is For...

Tuffers

Some of the stars who have played with and against Phil Tufnell get their retaliation in first!

Ian Botham

If Phil Tufnell had believed in himself he could have been a world-beater. Tuffers' problem has always been a lack of self-confidence, which will sound surprising to those people who believe the image of him as being a cocky Artful Dodger character. I have always rated Tuffers highly. He had flight, could turn the ball and possessed excellent control. There was no lack of talent.

He has certainly never conformed to the traditional idea of a professional sportsman. He had an aversion to such things as bleep tests; give him 20 Bensons, a couple of large ones and forty winks any day. When we first played together for England in 1991 we hit it off immediately. I found Tuffers friendly, witty and entertaining company. With his new found success recently on 'I'm a Celebrity, Get Me Out of Here' it sounds like a lot of the viewers did too. It is most certainly cricket's loss and television's gain.

Angus Fraser

It is with fondness that I look back on my 18 summers and four winters playing with Tuffers. He may have been a pain in the arse at times but life would be boring if we were all the same. This is an insult that could never be aimed at 'The Cat,'

Philip's life, and that of those who have taken an interest in it, has been like travelling on a blind roller-coaster ride. Nobody could predict what would happen from one week to the next and I do not see this changing. It is why anyone who meets him will always remember the occasion.

My memories start in 1985 when he drove into Lord's in a big old Volvo which had two stereo speakers on the rear window ledge. 'The Cat' had long hair, an earring and an attitude. The music blaring out was sung by Dead or Alive and Divine. Tuffers was in the Gothic stage of his life.

A Rover replaced the Volvo. Cars in Philip's life have always been an indication of how well his career has been going and it wasn't long before the Porsches and BMWs came along. A brush with the law forced him into a clapped out Fiesta but the new Jaguar suggests things are back on the up.

Pushing the pedals on the Rover in the late eighties were a notorious pair of crocodile skin shoes. I thought they were bloody awful but Tuffers loved them and felt they completed the look he was searching for. He wore them until there were holes in the sole.

On tour with England I struggled to keep up with him, all but a couple of thirsty colleagues did. My wife and I will never forget one Christmas Eve on England's tour to Australia in 1990/91. As a squad we went to a restaurant in Melbourne called the Aussie Fish Café. The wine flowed and we were all having a great time. As part of the evening's entertainment the waiters pulled the ladies from their tables and danced with them. Tuffers, feeling he could do better than this, jumped to his feet and picked a life-sized bust up off the bar. The display of dancing he put on had everyone in the restaurant in tears. It was a classic moment.

There are many more, but it is his book.

Mike Gatting

'The Cat' on and off the field was a very different creature, very intense on the field and very laid back off it. He could be brilliant yet frustrating, annoying yet funny and both quiet and noisy.

His brilliance showed against the West Indies at The Oval, possibly the highlight of his career, apart from many fine performances for Middlesex. The frustration he invoked on and off the field was bewildering, mystifying and extremely annoying.

His moods off the field were mainly good natured, funny and he was always very good company for the evening. Phil gave a lot of people a great deal of pleasure both on and off the field but I suspect he could have done more in his career.

Ronnie Irani

Phil Tufnell is aptly named 'The Cat,' Life's never dull when Phil is around. When he's bowling, he entices his prey by eyeing them up and often lulling them into a false sense of security before he pounces and claws them into his grasp, leaving the batsman ensnared and the bowler purring with pride.

A mischievous operator, he's made spin bowling an art form.

Off the field, the jack-the-lad persona masks a genuine and sincere personality who's a big-hearted full of fun guy and, with Phil, what you see is what you get. An appealing guy, both as a bowler pleading to the umpire for another victim and also as a character whose philosophy is to live life to the full.

Alan Lamb

Well, having the pleasure of playing cricket and touring a few countries with 'The Cat' has been quite an education both on and off the field!

'Cat' is normally a fairly quiet sort of character, a man of not many words, that is only when he is off the juice!

I remember captaining England in Adelaide against South Australia and we had a team meeting the night before to let the players know who was playing. Unfortunately 'The Cat' was not selected and I had to explain to him and others that they must make sure they were fit and healthy in case some team-mate went down ill.

"Not a problem," yelled 'The Cat' with a twinkle in his eyes, which was bad news. The following day going down to breakfast I bumped into him getting into the lift on the ground floor. I took one look at him and saw he was in a mess. Before I could saying anything 'The Cat' said, "Sorry skip, but I got held up in the casino and had a tri-vector." I asked what the hell that was!! He said, "Skip, I ended up with three casino girls in bed."

I warned him not to have a big night again as, I said, if the manager spotted him he would get a heavy fine. "Sorry skip, I won't do that again," he replied.

The following day Mickey Stewart and Peter Lush were on their way to breakfast and unfortunately bumped into 'The Cat' who again was the worse for wear. The management took one look at him and called a meeting. Poor Tuffers copped a heavy fine. But we did manage to keep it away from the press so the 'Cat' did not hit the headlines again.

Well Tuffers, King of the Jungle. It did not surprise me that he won. I have seen him eat worse things on tours!

Good Luck.

David Lloyd

What a hoot? I nearly fell off my dinner place when I saw 'The Cat' on that celebrity programme. I kept voting for him to get involved so to speak. Anything for a mate!!

He doesn't change does he? Terrific company and great fun. He can have his moments but can't we all... People in glasshouses and all that!

If you want a story, here's one that has never seen the light of day. England cricket team at fitness camp in Portugal, I'm in charge... thought they needed a night out... so took them line dancing... well, 'The Cat' took over the place!

If he is ever on TV get him to dance to Clarence Carter, better known as Dance Sleaze Slide... it will need censoring!

Robin Smith

There was a young laddie called Phil
Who most certainly knew how to chill
Yes, he slept quite a lot
Whether night time or not
But at cricket he also had skill

So our Tuffers, he bowled rather well
For his country 'n'll, bloody hell
Left-arm spin was his style
He shone out by a mile
Cos he bowled and the wickets, they fell

But when batting our friend found it tough
To be honest, the lad was a bit of a duff
Yes he thought he'd get hit
And got nervous as sh*t
But then calmed himself down with a puff

Yes, our Phil he enjoyed a good smoke
Having no ciggies left was no joke
He was once known to plead
Cos so great was his need
He just longed for a nice big fat toke

Then one day Phil 'The Cat' did this thing
That much fame and good fortune did bring
He ate beetles and stuff
He was hard, was our Tuff
Of the Jungle, our Phil he was King!

My mate Phil loved his wine and his beer
But he still had a damn good career
He was usually late
But was more than a mate
He was special, great fun, and sincere

Is For...

Aargh... Get Me Out of Here

Academy

Agnew

Allrounder

Ambidextrous

Antigua

Appealing

Arm Ball

Arse

Ashes

Ask

Athers

Audi

Average

Aargh... Get Me Out Of Here

When I announced my retirement one of the Middlesex lads said that I had been playing 'I'm A Cricketer, Get Me Out of Here' ever since he first met me. It is good to know your old team-mates hold you in such high esteem.

I've never really played the celebrity game but a chance to go on that show was too good to turn down once I knew I was not going to be turning the old arm over any more.

I was slightly surprised when the producers of the show told me I had to go and see a psychiatrist before they would let me loose with the creepy crawlies. After my experience with the shrinks a few years back I thought they must have been talking to Ray Illingworth. Luckily they said I was all there which is not what Illy would have thought. He would have asked for a second opinion.

And let's face it who is going to knock back the chance of a couple weeks in the sun with Catalina? Forget about the bugs, what a bird she is. Even if she reckons that cricket's boring.

It was certainly a bit different to playing at Canterbury or Chelmsford in April and a good bit warmer, even in the Australian autumn. You couldn't get me down there fast enough and a chance to do something good in Australia for once instead of getting carted.

As I said at the time you couldn't have better training for living in the jungle with a load of sweaty celebs than going on an England tour with a bunch of spotty-arsed cricketers.

Academy

There are two famous finishing schools in world cricket where the planet's finest cricketing talents are polished. First the Australian Academy of Sport in Adelaide, which has been responsible for Warne, Ponting, Lee and all those other world beaters who put the Aussies at the top of the world game. Second the Phil Tufnell Fielding Academy — which after my less than distinguished career in the schools of north London is about my only contribution to the education of the next generation.

A couple of fumbles in Sydney early in my first Ashes tour meant that when I arrived at the awesome Melbourne Cricket

Ground I was crapping myself enough without some Aussie putting a banner up in the stand with 'Phil Tufnell's Fielding Academy' scrawled all over it. Another one said, "Hey Tufnell, toss the ball to us and we'll throw it in for you." Charming — but it is all very easy from the comfort of the stands. The crowd don't know how hard it is to field in Australia. I blame the grass. The way the Aussies cut the grass in the outfield makes the ball wobble and it looked as though I'd been at the Foster's at breakfast.

More seriously, the English cricket authorities have finally woken up to the fact that it might be a good idea to get hold of our young cricketers during the off-season and coach them instead of letting them play charity football and pub darts in the Red Lion all winter.

We are just starting to see the fruits of Rod Marsh's appointment, with the first group of players who have been at the Academy achieving Test status. And some of them actually look and behave like professional athletes. Cricketers as athletes — what will they think of next?

I must admit I am glad it was not around in my junior days. My academy was the indoor school at Lord's followed up by a lengthy session in the Tavern next door bending the ears of the senior pros. A couple of the Middlesex lads were in the first intake to Marsh's prison camp and came back full of horror stories of cross-country runs, ice baths and non-stop fielding practice.

Apparently they were up at six for fitness training, then breakfast was followed by fielding drills, a trip to the gym, batting, warm-down and then a swim. Food was carbo-this and protein-that with not a drop of the local Shiraz in sight — which is a bit of a waste in the Adelaide area. And we worry about player burn-out. I'm surprised some of the boys made it up the steps of the plane to come home and start playing some cricket.

Agnew

Everyone is familiar with the voice of Jonathan Agnew, the BBC cricket correspondent, and his first ten years or so as a journalist coincided with my time as an international cricketer.

People largely forget what a great bowler he was for Leicestershire. He could always be relied on to get them 100 or so wickets a season and was unlucky not to play more than three times for England. When I first played county cricket Grace Road was a tough place to score runs with Agnew and Les Taylor steaming in and cutting the ball all over the place. But I bet he wished he was still playing the first time he interviewed me on the radio.

I had taken 7-46 in Christchurch and we had just won a Test against New Zealand that was tighter than a gnat's arse so the press boys wanted a few quotes with the man of the moment. The Kiwis could have saved the game and Martin Crowe knew that one decent blow would be enough for them to get a draw because there would not be enough time for the teams to turn round and for us to knock off the winning runs.

Anyway, Crowe knocked one of my gentle floaters up in the air only to see Derek Pringle cling onto it and we had won the game. The written press were a bit surprised that I didn't seem to know why Crowe had tried to launch me over the outfield but not half as shocked as Aggers was when he took out his tape recorder to have a word with me for the benefit of the listeners back in Blighty.

I was relaxed by now, the tension of the match had gone after a couple of gaspers and a tinny of the local brew, and Aggers opened up with, "Well Phil, that was an extraordinary performance. The New Zealanders didn't know how to play you at all."

"Yeah," I replied, "They was shittin' themselves." Apparently the interview needed all of the BBC's editing skills to be cleaned up to air on a family breakfast show. I think the Beeb have finally forgiven me. They actually let me loose with a microphone at the 2003 World Cup and now I've got my own radio show on Five Live.

Allrounder

A genuine Test class allrounder is about as rare as a batsman who walks nowadays because to be classified as an allrounder a player must be able to hold down a place in the side on batting or bowling alone. Ian Botham could have done it, Kapil Dev possibly and Imran Khan as well.

By definition a bowler who bats a bit can't be classed as an allrounder even in one-day cricket. There's only one around at the moment — Jacques Kallis of South Africa. Although Freddie Flintoff's form tells me he might be getting there.

Ambidextrous

When the Aussie boss John Buchanan was coach at Middlesex he was a great one for thinking out of the box but I thought he was out of his box when he said cricketers will soon be bowling and batting left and right-handed.

Now the Aussies have got bored with beating everyone playing one way round they want to see if they can do it cack-handed. On the batting front it is hard enough maintaining an average above six one way let alone doing it left-handed and imagine Warnie bowling normally then marking out a long run and serving up some vicious left-arm seam. Some baseball batters can, as it were, swing both ways but in glorified rounders hitting the ball is pretty easy and you don't need to move your feet too much. If I decided to switch to batting left-handed as the bowler ran up I would end up arse over tit and covered in nasty bruises. It doesn't bear thinking about or do much for your street cred.

And if bowlers have to tell the umpire which arm they are using wouldn't batsmen have to declare which way round they were batting? If they have to do that then the reverse sweep would become illegal. Mike Gatting would not be the only Englishman who wished they had outlawed the shot before the 1987 World Cup final.

Antigua

There are times on tour when you are at your wit's end with the endless plane journeys, different hotels and chasing leather for Brian Lara but a trip to Antigua soon shakes the dust out of your nostrils.

In these parts Viv Richards is king, and no wonder, with Curtly Ambrose prince and the entertainment is provided by the cross-dressing Gravy (see later) and Chicky's disco.

The Recreation Ground, where Brian Lara made his 375, is up there with Eden Gardens for atmosphere and the music which

Chicky blares out from an old wooden stand makes the place buzz like a club in Harlesden. The people are crazy about cricket and Chicky even turns his reggae tunes down when the bowler starts his run-up. Nice touch. In Lara's match there in 1994 Chicky even added 'Swing Low, Sweet Chariot' to his play-list for the odd time when England looked like getting on top. His disc is still in almost perfect nick because we were only in it for about 20 minutes before BCL came in. In the same match, which we saved thanks to tons from Mike Atherton and Robin Smith, I thought the Judge was going to dive for cover when he reached his 150.

He had had a tough tour and had copped some flak from the management who said he had too many interests away from cricket. But even he did not arrange the fly-past. After the Tiger Moth incident in Australia a couple of years earlier Judge was a bit wary of things flying overhead and I thought he was going to wet himself as a Jumbo Jet came in over the ground and buzzed him as he got to the landmark. You couldn't arrange that at Lord's.

Appealing

Spending all afternoon with your arms in the air and screaming like a madman would not appeal to everyone. But to us bowlers it is an essential part of the job. If you don't appeal you don't get anyone out and if you sometimes chuck in a dodgy shout when you know the batsman hasn't nicked it then it's all part of the game.

There have been some great appeals over the years from Richard Hadlee's single raised finger to my own personal favourite that is not so much a request as a plea for mercy.

Warnie's is a blinder especially when he has been bowling around the wicket with an unsympathetic umpire. He goes back on his haunches with both arms raised and a glazed look in his eyes, TELLING the umpire that this one really has pitched on the stumps, it's his googly and has done enough to hold its line. The batsman is not just out, he's plumb. It is Warnie's theory that every ball of his that hits the pad is out and just because the umpire can't pick his wrong 'un doesn't mean the batsman should detain him any longer.

There are some who just can't be bothered to go through the rigmarole of appealing. Instead, at the slightest hint of an edge, they are off charging down the pitch like a stampeding buffalo to high five with the slip cordon. The umpire surveying the carnage and a batsman with his jaw on the floor protesting his innocence takes sadistic pleasure in shaking his head and making the bowler trudge all the way back to his mark. Viv Richards went through a spell of appealing like this and virtually ended Rob Bailey's Test career by conning an umpire.

England took not bothering to appeal to another extreme on the Ashes tour in 2002-3. With someone like Steve Waugh you only get about half a dozen chances a decade so to not bother to appeal after he has nicked it straight to the keeper seems a bit odd. The ball from Geordie paceman Steve Harmison was heading towards second slip when James Foster caught it but no one appealed because apparently the Barmy Army were making too much noise and no-one heard the edge. The fact that it had moved about two feet after passing the bat didn't seem to come into it. Either Harmison had started swinging the ball like Waqar Younis or we had decided it would be best if Mister Waugh was left at the crease. It puzzled smarter cricket brains than mine.

Arm Ball

One of the most lethal deliveries in the book and one of the most overused by mediocre spinners. Some spinners are so proud of the one that goes straight on they bowl six of them an over. There are some bowlers on the circuit, with Test caps in their locker, who have never turned a ball off the straight in their lives.

But if you're turning it square it's worth slipping in one that goes straight on occasionally to keep the batsman on his toes. Instead of holding the ball across the seam you hold it like a seamer would so it drifts into the batsmen's legs.

When the arm ball comes off it is one of the most satisfying moments in cricket. The batsman who has been playing for the turn over after over is made to look like a prize pillock as the ball thumps into his pads and he's plumb in front of all three.

Most victims walk, complaining that they "played for the turn but it didn't go" without owning up to the fact that they have been done up like a kipper by a superb piece of bowling. They spend all afternoon making the bowlers look like mugs until being undone by the easiest ball to bowl in the coaching manual. Lovely.

Arse

Sometimes you can get distracted at the more picturesque grounds by a fit bird walking around the boundary but strangely you are more likely to hear fielders talking about batsmen's arses. And they are not all on the turn.

When a batsman doesn't fancy the quick stuff and starts backing away towards the square leg umpire you'll hear the call go up, "You've got him Curtly/Waz/Goughie — his arse has gone." Meaning his bottle has gone west and he would rather be back in the pavilion than wearing a couple of bouncers on his body.

Ashes

The contents of the little urn in the museum at Lord's are not the only Ashes you'll run into in that corner of London. Plum Warner, the former President of the MCC and England captain, had his remains scattered where he hit his first boundary at the ground and the ashtrays are always full in the dressing rooms. But the ones in the museum are the most famous and a series against the Aussies is still the ultimate to be involved in for an Englishman. We could be the worst two sides in the world, and let's face it the Aussies were pretty weak in the mid-eighties, but that would not make it any less important.

The Ashes might have been a bit one-sided in the past decade but for an Englishman it is the highest challenge. Some Aussies were saying before England's last trip down there that playing in India was more important to them — but that's crap and they know it. Playing Australia away is even better than playing them at home. The cricket is tough and although you might cop a bit of stick from the crowds, the entertainment at the end of the day's play is more than worth a bit of lip from a mouthy local. The food, the wine and the banter are just about the best you will find on any England trip and explains why more than 10,000 Barmies make the long haul down under.

Melbourne, for instance, is said to have more nightclubs per head than anywhere else in the world and I've been on the guest list at most of them. According to the blurb, the city is Australia's bar capital and some of the music venues took me back to my teenage days as an earring wearing punk in Highgate. The 'relaxed' attitude to drinking hours led to several early morning runs back to the hotel on my first trip, dodging the joggers and keeping my eyes firmly to the ground to avoid Goochie who was doing his early morning half marathon at the time I was creeping back to crash out for an hour or two before breakfast. The tour fee took a bit of a battering as well, from fines and extensive bar tabs.

For a red-blooded tourist the suburb of South Yarra was a bit of a shock — it is the centre of Melbourne's gay scene and more than once I had to make a hasty exit from some dodgy club when I realised the object of my drunken desire was sporting a six o'clock shadow.

England boys on tour often get accused of not mixing with the locals and shutting themselves in their hotel rooms and ordering room service when they are not at the ground. In Australia I can honestly plead not guilty on that charge.

Ask

A big favourite of the ex-pros in the commentary box these days, especially the Aussies. Apparently batting for two days on a raging bunsen to save a game against Murali is a big ask. Knocking off 35 runs in 15 overs is not.

Athers

Big respect to Athers for all he's done for me and my fellow tailenders over the last ten years. It takes a special bloke to make the sacrifices he has, surviving hours at a time while the opposition quicks enjoy a spot of legalised stoning. And he has not had medium pace trundlers trying to decapitate him. There are former England openers around with higher averages than Ath who managed to avoid some of the best and quickest bowlers of their generation by ducking out of tours at certain times but you can't accuse Athers of ever bottling a challenge. Walsh and Ambrose, Donald and Pollock, Wasim and Waqar, McGrath and Gillespie — it's enough to make a strong man turn to drink.

He was my offensive lineman, the bloke in American football who stops the quarterback from getting lynched by putting his own body in the line of fire. By the time I came in the bowlers were too knackered and the ball too soft to inflict much lasting physical damage. Most of the time. Occasionally the opposition got so riled by him staring straight back with that thin smile on his face they were steaming when the bunnies came into bat and they fancied some cheap wickets to bump up their figures. And let me tell you a pumped up Curtly Ambrose is the last bloke you want to see sprinting in from the other end with the second new ball in his hand. Cheers Ath.

If you add on over 50 Tests as captain, a dodgy back and dodgy guts from all the painkillers he took it's no wonder he looked knackered at The Oval in his last game. I couldn't believe it when Fred Titmus came out and had a go at him when he passed Peter May's record for skippering England in the most Tests. Cricket is a different game now and to survive as long as Athers did when the flak was flying almost non-stop was incredible.

When he was in charge the opposition bowled five per cent quicker at him, never holding anything back. They knew he was the main man and the big wicket so they never gave him an inch and he never gave them one back — look at the duel he had with Courtney Walsh in 1994 and the one with Alan Donald in 1998.

In the end the captaincy got to him, endless hassle, rounds of press conferences and England were not doing that well. We all blubbed a bit when he gave it up at the end of the West Indies tour in 1998 but you can see why he did. Sometimes captaining England must feel like pushing piss uphill. He led from the front and a lot of the time there was nothing to back him up. But the ovation he got from the crowd when he scored a hundred in the first Test after his resignation shows how much the public thought of him.

Not a lot of people know that it was down to me that Athers' reign as England captain lasted as long as it did. He was all set to chuck it in at The Oval in 1997, the only Test of that summer I played after being picked in all the squads and being told to sod off on the morning of the match.

Athers had backed Robert Croft all summer but apparently Wasim Akram, of all people, was championing my cause. Waz and Athers were big mates at Lancashire and by all accounts the big Pakistani swinger managed to sway the boss round to his way of thinking, and I was in. For once in his life Athers had been worn down by an opening bowler and the rest as they say is history. The Aussies slogged me up in the air and Athers stayed on in the job.

The way he retired from the game was typical. No fanfare, no fuss, no need to buy his round at the bar. He didn't even announce it in his Sunday newspaper column although all the press boys had sprinted to buy the first editions at Kings Cross Station.

Now he is a media pundit — one of many to cross the fence when they have called it quits on the field. Funny how people change — in his first Test on the box he said more than he did in over ten years with England.

It is not widely known that England's longest serving captain has no sense of smell. This is why he has gone on for over a decade facing the quickest stuff that Walsh and co. can throw at him — because he can't smell 'de leather' as it hurtles past his nose. Having a captain who can't smell has its drawbacks if you change next to him as I have done. When you had been leather chasing for two days in India or some other hotspot he sometimes needed a gentle prod that it was time to hit the launderette.

We did have a bit of a run-in in Jamaica once when I was catching up with some kip on the first morning of the Test instead of watching the action. As Alec Stewart and Athers were caning the Windies quicks to all parts I was fast asleep on the physio's couch.

To say I was bollocked by the skipper when he came in at lunch would be an understatement — he gave me both barrels and I suppose he had a point. Even though I was not playing it did not look good but as all the other lads were napping in the afternoon I was just getting my shuteye in early.

Despite the times when we didn't see eye to eye, those in the know tell me that most of the time he batted for me in selection meetings. In his book he admitted that he cut me a bit more slack than the other lads because he reckoned I could bowl no matter what was going on in my sometimes turbulent personal life. Which was nice.

Audi

Not a prize for Man of the Match in a one-day international on the sub-continent. Two noughts on the spin and you've bagged a pair. Four and you have an Audi. Five in a row is an Olympic — and the answer is yes.

Average

Apparently someone once said that there are lies, damned lies and statistics. Well, averages tell some of the biggest porkies going. They don't take into account who the opposition is, what the pitch is like or in the case of the overworked bowler how many catches have been grassed by hungover team-mates. Word of advice lads, if you have been on the sauce and you spot three balls coming at you at first slip go for the one in the middle — I've been doing it for years at mid-on and am pretty sure no-one has twigged.

At the end of the year when they publish the full list of stats in the posh rags only you know how much effort has gone into achieving the modest return of 35 wickets at 50 apiece when some nobody has just handed in 90 wickets at 20. The wicket of a short-sighted number 11 is given exactly the same importance as getting Viv Richards on a flat one at The Oval when the Master Blaster has been tucking in all afternoon. He should count as three wickets.

The way they work out batting averages proves that batsmen really do run the game. They get away with murder in the accounting department. How can a not out triple century against a load of students in April be used in the end of season divvy-up?

Is For...
Bails
Ball on a String
Ball Tampering
Barmy Army
B&B
Benaud
Benefit
Betting
Bichel
Bird
Bob's Bistro
Bondi Beach
Botham
Breakfast
Bumble
Bunny
Bunsen
Butcher

Bails

If the wind had been blowing in the right direction in Antigua in 1994 we would have got Brian Lara out for a mere 365 instead of 375. When he hooked Chris Lewis for four to get off 365 and go past Garry Sobers' mark his foot hit the stumps and the bail lifted up without falling off. Look at the picture — we could have got off lightly.

Ball on a String

If batsmen are allowed to have their little catchphrases like 'in the zone' then why can't bowlers? This is my favourite.

When the ball feels like it's on a string then I know I am bowling well and can virtually pitch it wherever I want to. It was like that when I got seven for 40-odd against New Zealand and the same against the Aussies at The Oval in 1997, but it can go tits up at times.

You might know where you should be putting the ball to a certain batsman but whatever you try you just can't make the bastard thing land where you want it to. Then it is not so much 'ball on a string' as on a long piece of knicker elastic.

Some of the top batsmen try and make you pitch the ball where they want it by faking to give you the charge then smacking you off the back foot when you've dropped it short. That doesn't look great and it looks a bit shabby when they play you really late from the crease like some of the Indian boys do. Sachin Tendulkar and Brian Lara are masters at this and can make fools out of the best twirlers on the circuit.

Ball Tampering

When the ball tampering row erupted people reacted as if it had never happened before in the history of cricket. All the old boys were wheeled out, spluttering into their pink gins and calling for life bans as if cheating had never existed.

W. G. Grace was famous for pulling strokes, but he was just a 'character' — suddenly the people who gave the ball a bit of treatment were no better than mass murderers. It has been going on for years but if it was done 30 years ago the bowlers were rascals rather than the out and out cheats they are labelled now.

Batsmen are using four pound bats with springs in and the poor old bowlers can't put a bit of work in on the seam. The ball is our only tool and we can't do anything about it. I am not saying the quicks should be allowed onto the pitch with machetes to gouge lumps out of the ball (most of them are dangerous enough as it is without encouraging them) but there should be a bit of leeway. You can shine the ball on your strides but can't put a bit of dirt on it to get it to reverse (of which more later).

The most effective method of ball tampering I have found is bowling to someone like Adam Gilchrist or Viv Richards. The ball soon loses its shine after it has bounced off the top of the stands a couple of times or landed on the beach about 300 yards away.

Athers bore the brunt of the flak in England for the 'dirt in pocket affair' in 1994 and nearly lost his job over it but he was not the only person in the world 'altering the condition of the ball.'

The way the authorities handled the situation was straight out of an Ealing comedy with Athers even offering his trousers to the men in suits so they could have a butchers at his pockets. At the time he said he would sue anyone who called him a cheat and surprise, surprise, no one did.

It had been going on for years and he was slaughtered after being spotted by the TV cameras. Using a bit of dirt on the ball was a big no-no but using Brylcreem was a bit of a lark. What utter crap.

Barmy Army

For most of my Test career the England side was surrounded by the Barmy Army, the bunch of lads and lasses who follow us all over the world. For such a bad tourist I have played much more Test cricket away from England than at home so most of it has been in front of these loons. They come from all walks of life, lawyers, builders you name it... but they have one thing in common — a love of English cricket, sinking a few cold ones and having a laugh in the sun.

And they are all ages, from kids just out of school enjoying the cricket in a year off to Jack Hyams, who, at the age of 79, spent an Ashes tour travelling around Australia in a yellow 1984 Ford Falcon estate — madness.

There were a few diehards watching us in Jamaica and Guyana at the start of the 1994 tour to the West Indies but by the time we arrived and won in Barbados the rumshops were more like English pubs than Caribbean watering holes.

It gives you a great lift to walk out on the first day of a Test match 10,000 miles away from home and see the flags waving. Then it dawns on you. These people have taken probably their only holiday of the year, or even given up their job, while spending piles of their hard earned dosh, to come and see you play cricket. And you don't want to let them down.

After all they would put down their beers and swap places with you at the first opportunity so you can't fail to be inspired by their dedication. It is a shame they did not have more to celebrate in my career bar the odd isolated win when the main business of the series was over.

They spice up the nightlife too. The best and biggest nights out are after a win abroad in somewhere like Adelaide or Bridgetown. By the time you have got all the formalities out of the way at the ground, picked up your man of the match award (in my dreams) and made your way to the nearest bar, the fans are absolutely shedded after being on the light ales all day. After we beat the Aussies in Adelaide in 1995, the Barmies went crazy and an all-nighter followed. They'd had a ten-hour headstart on us lads on the pitch so naturally we owed it to them to try and catch up.

And it is not all sunburn and beers. On the most recent trip to Australia they raised about £20,000 for cancer research.

Even more barmy recently was the way they goaded Brett Lee by calling no-ball every time he bowled — a clear reference to the work he has had done on his action.

Now, I love the Barmies to bits but I am just glad I was on that tour in a social capacity only. Winding up the world's quickest bowler, with the tail in, on a pitch that is cracking fast is just, well, barmy.

B&B

Whenever a wicket is as flat as a fart, with the sun beating down on it, you can bet your last Benson that some ex-player (usually a batsman) in the press box will come out with "So-and-so should be booking in for bed and breakfast on this one."

Speaking as someone who has never even booked in for 40 winks while batting, let alone bed and a full English, the thought of seeing the same bloke down the other end of the track patting the ball back at you all day is enough to drive you mad.

When Lara got his 375 against us I never thought we would see the back of him until we had to get the plane home from Antigua airport. Even then I had to check my luggage to make sure he wasn't in there.

Bed and breakfast is also a big factor when you look at the fixture list at the start of the county season so you can work out when you want your mid-season break. A bad experience in some dingy B&B can cause all sorts of mystery illnesses the next year when the same fixture comes around.

Benaud

Richie Benaud is the voice of cricket and God knows how they are going to replace him when he finally calls it a day in 2005. Did you ever notice how there was no fuss when Channel Four got the contract to show England's Test matches in 1999? (Their decision not to show World Cup highlights is another matter). No letters from disgusted colonels because of the adverts between overs or because of their different style of coverage. They had Richie and that was that.

They announced the contract and then that Benaud would be leading the commentary team so there were no arguments. As long as Benaud was in the box they could have been showing a ten-over slog between a couple of pub sides.

He hasn't risen to his God-like status in the press box without knowing what he is talking about but he was stretching it a bit when he compared me to the Australian rugby winger David Campese.

In Adelaide on the 1994-5 tour I took a catch to dismiss

Michael Slater which should have put all the fielding academy jibes to bed once and for all. If Jonty Rhodes had taken it they would still be playing it on the box. The Barmy Army went well and truly barmy because it put us on the road to a win and Benaud claimed that the goose step I took as I clung onto the catch was straight out of Campo's manual. In truth I was crapping myself so much as it came down to earth I was trying to dry off my strides by jogging around and getting a bit of ventilation in downstairs.

Benefit

A large tax-free wedge of the folding stuff obviously comes in handy when retirement and a life of commentary and crown green bowls beckons, but the real enjoyment from having a benefit year comes from the 12-month stretch of dinners, golf days and race nights. It is like going on a year-long stag do with a bit of cricket chucked in.

And by the end of the year you are 99 per cent certain to be single again because as soon as the missus sees the cash piling up in your joint account the first thing she does is file for divorce and at least half of your hard-earned nest egg. My benefit was in 1999, divorce followed in 2001. All you have to show for the slog around the shires is an enlarged liver and a reduced bank balance. It is the same for every player.

Some county pros cop a lot of stick for 'hanging on for a benefit and blocking the way for youngsters,' Well, if any of the Middlesex young spinners had wanted to take me out for a year-long beano they could have had my place in the side long before I chucked it all in.

Alternative: What county cricketers have to claim in the winter if they can't find work as a bouncer or coaching overseas. When you roll up to the DSS office at the end of the season pleading poverty the bird behind the ramp always opens with "And why did you leave your last job, sir"?

To which you can only reply, "It is November, I've been bowling my nuts off all summer but the selectors don't fancy my chances of rolling over Sachin Tendulkar on a road in Calcutta."

Some of the heftier lads supplement their giros with a spot of cash-in-hand bouncing outside dodgy nightclubs and many is the time I have been stopped from going into some dingy nightspot in London by a South African quickie trying to pay for his fare back to Cape Town.

Betting

People claim that Middlesex and England paid me for getting nought for more than 15 years but I can honestly say I was never approached to throw a match or bowl badly. Actually, if matches are being fixed as often as people say I'm a bit miffed no-one thought I could do my bit in return for a few quid or a leather jacket. I've been in enough dressing rooms and like to think I am streetwise enough to know if there's anything a bit iffy going on. Then again I thought Hansie Cronje was whiter than white.

Some of the names they have come up with are bizarre. A quick look at the stats shows names like Warne, Waugh and Lara don't underperform anywhere. They might like a punt at the races but there are not going to throw a match for a few extra quid. And the rules on betting on cricket are quite clear now. You can't even bet on a game in your garden with your daughter opening the batting.

People have said we should cancel so-called meaningless one-day tournaments but such things don't exist. Joe Public might think some of the competitions are Mickey Mouse but the players don't — they care and they remember the results. A five-for against the Aussies is a five-for against the Aussies if it is taken in Sydney, Sharjah or Southgate.

But the whole thing does make you think about your own stats. When their number three hits you up in the air to mid-on was it a mindless slog, had he been wedged up or was it a brilliant piece of bowling frustrating him into a bad shot?

Was the half-volley that scorched off the middle of your bat and thumped into the boundary boards deliberate or had your fancy footwork put the bowler off his length? All that preys on your mind. You need to know that everyone is busting a gut to win because if they're not it takes the shine off everything you have worked so hard to achieve.

Bichel

The rise and rise of Andy Bichel during the 2003 World Cup was the perfect illustration of why Australia are so far out in front of everyone else. Admit it, before the tournament most people thought of him as an honest journeyman pro instead of a world beater but as soon as they had a few injuries he stuck his hand up.

Don't forget they won the tournament without Shane Warne and Jason Gillespie, and Bichel was the difference.

The big occasion inspired him as he took seven wickets and scored vital runs against England. When was the last time an English second-stringer took his chance in the team like that? They are a different breed.

Bird

The sight of the world's most famous umpire, Harold 'Dickie' Bird, walking out to the middle was enough to strike fear into the hearts and hamstrings of all bowlers and suncream salesmen everywhere. Although the boys selling umbrellas outside the ground were always quids in if Dickie was on duty.

In his playing career Dickie was a batsman for Yorkshire and Leicestershire and as they say once a batsman always a bloody batsman. I always tried to get on at the opposite end to Dickie because you had to be knocking all three out before bothering to appeal. Once I gave him one of my best screams, arms up, eyeballs bulging, squatting down, pleading with him to give me a decision. All I got was a startled, "Don't shout at me like that, don't shout — I can't give that out, I can't give it." It is rumoured that he used to wake up in the middle of the night screaming "not out."

So batsmen had to be 100 per cent to be out which is fair enough if the umpire is consistent and Bird was consistent — it was consistently not out.

He always reminded me of some old mother hen clucking over her chicks when he was panicking on the field and as an ex-pro he had a great affinity with the players. As with all good umps he set the mood of the day when he was in charge.

His effect on the weather was notorious — he has even suspended play for good light and a burst water pipe on the pitch in his time. Once a game which Dickie was umpiring in 1976 between Derbyshire and Lancashire at Buxton was halted because of — of all things — snow.

At the first sign of a cloud he would start clucking, making sure the groundsmen were in place to pull the covers on, even if the ground was bathed in glorious sunshine.

In his final Test match at Lord's in 1996 between England and India he even gave Athers out LBW to Javagal Srinath in the first over of the game. Dickie had only just wiped the tears away from his eyes after a presentation before play and within minutes he was giving the England captain his marching orders. All Athers could do was grin — given out LBW by Dickie Bird in his last Test match — now that one must have been plumb.

Bob's Bistro

Probably the highlight of the 1993 trip to India was seeing tour manager Bob Bennett togged up like a chef knocking out corned beef hash for the lads. The night before the second Test in Madras, which was going to be tough enough anyway, Goochie and Gatt had a Chinese in the hotel restaurant, a meal which included the most famous bowl of prawns in history. Both of them were reduced to shivering wrecks by a dose of Gandhi's Revenge that left Gooch in the hotel at the start of the game and Gatt back in bed spewing by lunch.

They got a lot of stick for eating them but we had had a lot of seafood on the trip and no-one came down with anything like this. The sight of the England captain and the best player of spin we had going green forced Bennett into action.

Bob's Bistro was born. For the rest of the tour we were fed a diet of corned beef, baked beans and nan bread prepared by Bennett, physio Dave Roberts and the chaplain Andrew Winfield-Digby. It certainly wasn't going to win any Michelin stars and by the end of the tour I was sick of it.

Alec Stewart took this all so seriously that when he went to India again for the World Cup all he ate was chicken breasts brought from home. He was counting down the days left by the number of bits of meat he had left to get through. He is always clucking behind the stumps like some old mother hen but by the time he got home he was laying eggs.

Bondi Beach

After a few years of watching Aussie soaps during the frequent rain breaks when I started out on the county treadmill I was gagging to get down to Bondi Beach for a bit of sly leching when I first arrived in Sydney.

I thought a spot of body surfing should be enough to ingratiate myself with the local lovelies and then it would be game on, or so I thought. Although it has been cleaned up now it is hard to put on a show for the opposite sex when you're always dodging turds and used syringes.

If this wasn't bad enough I got dumped by a wave which separated me from my luminous Speedos and forced me to withdraw, not so gracefully, with my tail between my legs after drawing a rare blank on the crumpet front.

Botham

You have to feel a bit sorry for Beefy. All the old videos and pictures of him slaughtering the opposition in his heyday also show him with the worst hairstyle in the western world – the bleached blonde mullet. For a few years no one was brave enough to tell him how crazy it looked but someone must have plucked up the courage eventually. Probably Mrs B.

Imagine him showing the video of Brisbane 1986 to his grandchildren – they would not be able to take their eyes off his ridiculous barnet flowing in the breeze as he launched Merv Hughes for another boundary.

But for my generation he was the man. On and off the field. Smashing the Aussies all over the park before drinking them under the table – what a hero. He once dismissed his innings at Headingley in 1981 as a bit of a freak. I wish I'd had a couple of freaks like that.

But before that game he was ignored by all the members at Lord's in his last match as captain and Beefy never forgets. From

Being in the jungle was more boring than watching the rain fall at Headingley (photos: Granada)

Another scalp for Curtly Ambrose as Ian Botham famously fails to get his leg over at the Oval in 1991

"In my day..." "No, in my day..." - Ray Illingworth and Geoff Boycott discuss the finer points of cricket

A dodgy back and a dodgy hamstring, but Mike Gatting could still bat a bit

then on he refused to acknowledge the applause from that end of the ground when he had his Superman kit back on. As a bit of a rebellious teenager at the time I thought it was brilliant.

He was the first rock star of cricket and the attention he got from the press makes my brushes with the tabloids look almost insignificant. Despite his massive aura he always had time for people he thought were good blokes and luckily he seemed to think I was all right.

I owe Beefy a big drink for making me feel at home in the England set-up and proving you don't have to be a robot to play Test cricket. When I got back into the side for The Oval Test in 1991 I had not played a Test all summer after being branded a naughty boy on the Australian tour the winter before.

I was a bit uneasy when I arrived at the ground and there was minimum chat. I thought, "Bloody hell that's nice. I know everyone in the room and no-one is talking to me." So I just sloped around with a permanent fag on.

All quiet until Botham arrived. He doesn't walk into the room, it's more of a stampede and he announced his arrival by slamming two bottles of Aussie red on the table and shouting, "These are for the first guy to get a hundred." If he had been talking about bowling figures I would have been even happier.

He approached me with an outstretched paw, crushed my spinning finger and welcomed me back into the fold with "How you doing Cat, me old mate?"

One minute of Botham and I felt I was back.

I am not sure that Athers wants to see Botham in a bar again though. Apparently after his 185 that saved the game against South Africa at the Wanderers Beefy challenged him to a rum and coke challenge that went on until Athers could hardly stand. After eleven hours being pummelled by Allan Donald and Shaun Pollock the last thing you need is a night out with Beefy.

Not a bad player either. A Test allrounder should be capable of holding his place in the side as a batsman and as a bowler and there are not many people who can do that. Most allrounders have a strong suit but the Beef could have got into the side as a bowler or a batsman alone. If he had given up bowling when his back went he could have batted number three but he didn't want to because he had to be involved in every minute of the game — he would drive the skipper mad trying to get a the ball in his hands or be put up the order.

In the 1992 World Cup he was virtually a cripple when we played the Aussies at the SCG but seeing our oldest enemy run out really fired the old boy up.

Off a five pace run-up and bowling at about my pace Beefy took four wickets for no runs in seven balls. The ball that got Border LBW hardly made it to the other end. The Aussies did not know what had hit them and were like rabbits in headlights as they committed hari-kari in front of 60,000 smashed fans.

With Botham opening the batting and the target only 172, I did not even bother to get my pads out of my coffin and he did not disappoint as he smashed them all over the park. Awesome.

He proved you could enjoy yourself and still play tough cricket and his attitude to nets was right up my street. If your average was calculated by dividing runs scored by hours slept the night before Both would be up there with Bradman.

He did not stop when he retired either. He's raised millions for charity with his walks and has seen off a small army of people who have tried to keep up with him on the road and in the bar. David Lloyd used him in an advisory role a few years ago with the England team and the boys really listened to him because he was their hero when they started playing the game. Although it is good to have him around in the commentary box it would be better if he was more involved with running the England set-up.

Breakfast

You get to stay in some top notch hotels these days when you are away with England which must cost the board a fortune and it is money well spent. But as far as I'm concerned they could skip the breakfast.

When I woke up on the day of a Test I felt sick with nerves and the last thing I wanted to do was to neck a full English or even a piece of cold toast. My guts were usually churning, my head was spinning and the most I could keep down was a fag and a cup of tea. Cricket may be the only sport that stops for meal breaks but before a day's play I couldn't stomach anything.

In India it was even worse. There is nothing more gut wrenching after a night on the local brew than to come down to breakfast and find the tables heaving with lime pickle and spicy scrambled eggs. Not the sort of thing they dish out on the motorways of England.

God knows what some of the big names have for breakfast before they go out but I can just imagine Curtly Ambrose digging into double egg, liver, bacon, sausage, kidneys, black pudding and hash browns before trotting out to knock someone's head off.

Bumble

If you think David Lloyd is enthusiastic in the Sky commentary box then you should have seen him in the England dressing room when he was coach. He is still in love with cricket and has seen it from all sides after spells as a player (with a Test double ton to his name), coach, selector and even as a First Class umpire.

One day I sidled up to him and told him I was not that keen on nets and took a pace back waiting for the fireworks. I didn't know what to say when he asked me just to do one session — so I said I would do two. I had been done up like a kipper and Bumble had fooled me into doing twice my normal workload. A victory for reverse psychology and a lesson to coaches everywhere. The big stick approach is not the only way to produce decent cricketers.

The dressing room when he was in charge looked like a primary school classroom with massive signs all over the place telling you what to do. He even managed to make training vaguely enjoyable by introducing games and new routines into our drills rather than let us plod round the boundary all day.

Mostly he left me alone and let me get on with my bowling but it was good to chat with him about tactics now and then. A lot of people had me down as a tactical half-wit but I do know a bit about the game and I enjoyed the chance to show it under Bumble. In one team meeting I was putting in my two-pennyworth and the lads clearly weren't paying attention to what I was saying so I screamed out "I'm f****** serious about this you know." The room went quiet but I think Bumble was secretly impressed that I was so passionate about my cricket.

He is not afraid to make a joke about himself either. He was famously 'boxed' by Jeff Thomson on that brutal tour to Oz in 1974-5 and after the blow at Perth he was picking out plastic from his wedding tackle for a couple of weeks. He said his protector had been turned inside out — not leaving much room for anything to go inside it.

When he copped another blow there from the Middlesex seamer, and now a distinguished member of the press corps, Mike Selvey a few years later he was doubled up again. Selve asked about his health and Lloyd came back quick as a flash with "After Thommo you were a pleasure."

When you have been hit by Thomson you are not going to be worried about a few redneck Zimbabweans and I doff the Tufnell titfer in recognition of his bravery when we were in Harare.

One of the stands next to our dressing room housed some very loud, very drunk spectators who kept lobbing bottles onto the floor. They would neck a beer and sling the empty down close to the boundary where the black waiters would have to pick it up. As the afternoon wore on and the beers kicked in they would start throwing them at the waiters.

Bumble hates this sort of thing and had obviously had a brave pill with his lunch so he went over and picked up a bottle, marched up to the biggest bloke in the stand who must have weighed in at about 20 stone and asked him if he'd dropped something. They went ballistic and I thought that was the last we would see of our boss but somehow he lived to tell the tale.

Bunny

Bunnies in a cricketing sense are not the rather attractive young females who look after you in a lap dancing club following a day of hard toil in the field but an opposing batsman who you love bowling at and usually get out.

Before going out to field on the first day of a match I would always have a quick butchers down the opposition's batting line-up and tot up how many wickets I was going to get. If I recognised two or three of my bunnies in the list then I would dance down the pavilion steps ready to grab the ball off my skipper after the quicks had had a couple of overs.

On the flip side, if a couple of their batsmen have given you some tap in previous games and the captain looks like throwing you the ball then it is time for some delaying tactics. "He might as well have played me with a blindfold on last year Skip," usually holds him off for a few overs or even "They don't look like they like it up them," can earn you a few minutes thinking time while the captain keeps the speed merchants on.

I can't pretend I ever enjoyed bowling to Mark Waugh, he was one who could silently murder you although he always gave you a chance, but it would appear that Mr Waugh Jnr is my bunny. Last time I looked I had got him out seven times including once bowled for 99 at Lord's when the top three Aussie batsmen had all got tons. The bowler who has the honour of getting me out most times in Tests is not Curtly Ambrose or Glenn McGrath but Mr S.Warne who has seen me off four times. I don't think I'm the most prized scalp in his locker.

Bunsen

To non-cricketers the Bunsen burner is the metal thing in the chemistry labs at school that the teachers thoughtfully put out on the desks for you to light your fags with. But for spinners like me it is the Holy Grail.

Bunsen burner (turner) is cricketer speak for a wicket that will take a bit of spin so when your skipper says, "It's a raging bunsen Tuffers, you can fill your boots" you know you're under the cosh.

On a flat deck where the ball isn't doing anything no-one complains when you hand in a solid two for 60 after 25 overs of trying to keep the batsmen pinned down.

But on a bunsen if you get less than five-for zip you're

for the high jump. Conditions are all in the spinner's favour and you're expected to run through the oppo like a dose of Gandhi's Revenge. This brings it's own sort of pressure. If you haven't taken a wicket after five or six overs you start fretting and trying to bowl miracle balls that pitch a foot outside leg stump and hit the top of off. Still, it's better than bowling on the batsman-friendly roads that get dished up most of the time.

Butcher

I raised a glass or two to my old mate Butch when he got to three figures against the Zimbos at Lord's and nearly choked on my beer when he ran through their batting the next day. Test number three batsman I can swallow but he was almost being talked about as the Next (whisper it quietly) Botham.

Still it was great to see my old mucker with that cheesy grin on his face because he has been through the mill more than most without seeming to let it get him down.

He had his fair share of attention from the press for non-cricketing matters but was always the first to gee the lads up with a song or by buying another round. Just my sort of bloke.

He was mucked around by the selectors at the start of his career, a familiar tale for an England batsman, although he managed to avoid membership of the one-cap wonders club. Unlike his old man Alan.

With Butch they couldn't decide if he was a number three, six or opener, allrounder or the bloke who carries the drinks. Funnily enough it was when he was being pissed about by England by batting at number six that I really thought he had cracked it as a Test player.

On the 1998 tour of the Caribbean he went in at number three in Jamaica and it took Courtney Walsh precisely one ball to clean him up. A few minutes later the game was called off but unfortunately for Butch the grizzly stats are still in the book.

They say stats don't lie but on this occasion they are talking bollocks. What they don't say is that Viv Richards in his pomp would have struggled with Walsh's throat ball that day and that Butch had not held a bat in anger for about five months because of crap planning on the part of the, er, selectors. He only played in the match at all because Jack Russell was confined to the little boys' room with a dose of Montezuma's Revenge.

You don't get many second chances if you are an England player and Butch duly spent the next Test strumming his guitar on the pavilion balcony in Trinidad. He was back for the next game and saved our arses as we scraped home to level the series.

Coming in at six with 60-odd needed he inched us home. I was padded up in the dressing room shitting myself that I would have to go on with four needed and Curtly pawing the ground at the end of his run-up. Butch's 24 not out may not look like much in *Wisden* but to the boys in the England team that day it was worth as much as a big ton. As they say in the Windies — big up Butch.

Is For ...
Caddick
Cafeteria Bowling
Calling Card
Cap
Captaincy
Carry Your Bat
Caught Out
Ceefax
Central Contracts
Champagne Moment
Chuckers
Coffin
Collapse
Compton
Corridor Of Uncertainty
Corruption
County Cricket
Croft
Curtly And Courtney
Cut

Caddick

Caddy Shack was one of two so-called awkward customers brought back into the fold by Nasser Hussain when he took over as captain from Alec Stewart in 1999. As I was the other one, I prefer to think of us as being enigmatic rather than a pain in the arse.

On his day, when the wind is blowing in the right direction, Caddy can be the most lethal bowler in the country. If he doesn't fancy it then he gets spanked.

Twice against the West Indies in 2000 he had everything going in his favour. Bowling at the right end, wind in the right direction, running downhill and, most importantly, Gough steaming in from the opposite direction. Result — five for 16 at Lord's, five for 14 at Headingley and two England wins.

When Goughy was made English Cricketer of the Year after that series against the Windies he was quick to point out that he was not the same bowler without Caddy at the other end. The two of them are complete opposites on the pitch and dovetail nicely.

Caddy is about seven foot tall and bowls, as ex-trundlers like Gus Fraser would call it, back of a length and keeps batsmen in their crease. They don't like to step too far down the track in case they get one in the teeth. Goughy, on the other hand, bowls much fuller and is more in the market for LBWs and yorkers smashing into the base of the stumps. Between them they were the most successful England opening pair since the mighty Beef and Bob Willis were strutting their stuff in the late seventies and early eighties.

If you take Goughy out of the equation, though, Caddy can go into his shell and become half the bowler he is when the Yorkshire Rhino is charging in at the other end. He was slagged off a bit for not ripping the ball out of Nasser's hands during the game against Australia in the World Cup. The Aussies were reeling, then fought back and, with Michael Bevan and Andy Bichel still in, were pretty well set with a couple of overs left.

Instead of chucking the ball to the Caddy, who was sitting on four for 30-odd, Nas gave it to Jimmy Anderson who promptly got carted. The press had a field day saying that Caddy, as the senior bowler on the pitch, should have demanded he bowled the penultimate over. But he's not like that. Maybe he would have been a better bowler if he had a bit more devil in him.

His mouth gets him into trouble sometimes. He was once quoted as saying that he had worked out how to bowl to Brian Lara and he would have no trouble getting him out. Lara read that one and gave him the caning of his life. When he did get Mister Lara in Antigua, the maestro had 375 to his name and the send-off he got from Caddy made him piss himself. When a batsman has done that to you it is better to let him go quietly.

Off the pitch Caddy is the England team's Mr Fixit. He claims that he qualified as a painter and decorator in New Zealand before he came over to England and his father has some kind of building business over there.

He is certainly a dab hand with a screwdriver and if you need someone to tosh your living room or fix a bat then Caddy's your man. When he was not picked for one winter tour he took out his frustration on the Taunton fences and pavilion by giving them a quick dose of emulsion. Other players just went to the pub. I get a rash if I get near a computer but some of the boys have said that if your laptop's gone down he can fix that as well. Fairly handy bloke to have around.

Cafeteria Bowling

Gatt loved cafeteria bowling where you could literally help yourself to whatever runs you fancy. And, like the queue in the café, it was always better to get in front of Gatt if this type of bowling was on the menu. Also known as buffet bowling.

Calling Card

If your luck is in on tour then some bit of local skirt will surreptitiously slip her calling card under your hotel room door and hopefully you'll notice it before the cleaner gets into the room. Not as easy as it sounds as I often used the cleaner as my alarm call after a night on the tiles.

Fast bowlers also like to leave their calling cards. Usually on your body in the form of big bruises with dimples where the seam has hit your torso. Thank God for all the body armour we wear nowadays or I'd look like a prune with the amount of punishment I have taken. Some batsmen wear them like medals but I can't see the point of showing off the fact that you're not quick enough to get out of the way of a chest-high bouncer coming at you at 90 miles an hour.

Cap

Being capped by your county is one of the most significant moments in any player's career. You are now officially one of the boys and for most it means a significant hike in your wages so you don't have to worry about walking to grounds because you can't afford the tube fare. Once you have got your cap it is also very useful to pull over your face so the skipper can't catch your eye if he wants you field in close.

Captaincy

I've always fancied myself as a bit of a skipper. Broad shoulders for the lads to cry on, bags of experience, hard but fair, fearless in the line of fire, you know the sort of thing. Unfortunately no one else saw me as officer material.

And we all know that captains of cricket teams should always be bowlers because they think about the game so much more than batsmen. But historically the batters always get first dibs at tossing the coin before the match.

But imagine the epitaph: 'Phil Tufnell — the captain who beat the Australians,' Now that would not have been a bad way to begin and end my captaincy career.

Last time the Aussies were over I was down to skipper Middlesex against them in a one-day game at Lord's. That's right Phil Tufnell leading the Londoners against Warne, Waugh, Ponting, Gillespie etc. I couldn't wait.

Nice early night with a cup of cocoa so I would be in tip-top condition for the following day and a good night's sleep would put me right to face the old enemy. But when I woke up I felt like I'd been on one of Botham's nights out on tour. And looking back I wish I had been. Sweating, headache, dry mouth all that sort of thing and I realised I had flu — in June.

Paul Weekes took over the armband and did a great job as the lads beat the Aussies by six wickets and struck the first blow for England in their bid to undermine the confidence of the tourists.

I'd like to be able to say I was constantly on the blower giving Weekesy the benefit of my tactical mega-brain and my experience of routing the Australians but I'm afraid it was all down to him. So next time you are at a pub quiz and they ask who the last English captain was to beat the Aussies at Lord's you'll know the answer.

Carry Your Bat

You are always better off taking a bit of wood into the middle with you although Bob Willis managed to go out to bat in a Test match once without carrying his weapon out with him. If an opener carries his bat it means he is the last man standing when all the others have been dismissed. He is either a genius or can count to six so that when the tasty bowling is on he always makes sure he's up at the other end watching his partner suffer.

Caught Out

You are caught out in cricket when a picture of you and two scantily-clad Aussie birds appears on the front page of an English newspaper when you get back from tour.

Ceefax

The usual way of finding out what you are doing in the winter. Touring or stuck in Blighty.

Central Contracts

No one can seriously doubt that central contracts have made a real difference to the English cricket team. Since they were introduced an English new ball pairing, Darren Gough and Andy Caddick, actually lasted a whole summer against the West Indies without one of them having to be shot like a knackered racehorse, and we won the series. Not that it did their county sides, Yorkshire and Somerset, much good.

Members complain that some of their star names are not available for the whole summer but you can't have your cake and eat it, and if they want a successful England side then I'm afraid they have just got to bite the bullet. International cricket pays the bills for county cricket, not the other way round.

Look at the situation in Australia where the Test boys play for their state sides about as often as Glenn McGrath bowls a long-hop. Warnie has taken more wickets for Australia than he has for Victoria because of this but this doesn't make him any less of a player. The old boys carp on about getting fit to bowl by bowling in matches but these days I'm afraid it just doesn't stack up like that.

Having a couple of lads on England duty frees up some space in the county sides to develop youngsters and now with two foreign players allowed in each team there should always be some experienced, top-class cricketers around for the kids to tap up for advice.

The key to it is how the England side treat the players. Batsmen and slow bowlers need games more than the quicks. The batters in particular like any chance to make a few easy runs and up their average while spinners need a good bowl to get into a rhythm. Once the fast boys are fit however they just need to keep it ticking over and make sure they are fresh for the games that matter. And to Joe Public they are the Test matches.

The deals should just be given to the players who need a bit of looking after. It was pointless giving one to the Lancashire leg-spinner Chris Schofield a couple of years back and then tossing him back to Old Trafford.

I never had the offer of a central contract. I mean what would have been the point of paying me for the whole summer and then just picking me at The Oval? Even with my grasp of finances it's obvious that wouldn't make sense. It must be tempting, though, to bank the fat cheque at the start of the season and take it easy — perish the thought.

Champagne Moment

I've never earned enough as a cricketer to get too much of a taste for the fizzy stuff so it is nice to nick a bottle off the BBC occasionally. The odd bottle nicked from the sponsors' tents is about the most I normally manage.

But when Ramps got his first Test wicket — David Williams ct Tufnell 15 at Bourda in 1998 the lads in the commentary box thought we each deserved a bottle of bubbly for the Test Match Special Champagne Moment. In the words of one of their commentators, Christopher Martin-Jenkins in his report in Her Majesty's *Daily Telegraph*, "Tufnell took a brilliant catch diving to his right at square leg." They don't come along that often so they are worth remembering. Fortunately, though, champagne moments with members of the fairer sex are a more common occurrence.

Chuckers

As someone who was once accused of throwing in New Zealand I can fully appreciate how being labelled a chucker can affect your international career. So hats off then to Neil Smith who livened up the dreary 1996 World Cup with one of the most spectacular vomits ever seen in the history of the game.

He got his juices flowing in England's match against the United Arab Emirates in Peshawar when he opened the batting and then opened his throat to chuck the previous night's pizza onto the wicket. And he threw up to the umpire's right so that any left-armers would have to go round the wicket or wade through a semi-digested American Hot as they delivered the ball. Good thinking Smithy, but fancy going all the way to Peshawar for a pizza and then throwing it up. Didn't seem to do his prospects at the highest level that much good either.

Dean Jones set the ball rolling on the chucking front when he deposited his breakfast on the side of the pitch in Madras in 1986. Apparently Allan Border wandered down the other end and told Jones that if he wasn't up to the job he would get someone else out there instead. Typical Aussie, Jones scored a double ton and then spent a couple of days on a drip in Madras General Hospital before coming back for the next game.

Phil DeFreitas did the business once on England duty. He overloaded at the drinks break and chucked up all over the umpire's back as he was running in to bowl. My favourite Daffy memory.

More recently, the Indian left-armer Ashish Nehra celebrated taking six wickets and virtually knocking England out of the World Cup by producing a superb display of vomiting. Down on one knee, spewing his guts and isotonic drink all over the strip at Durban. I've felt like throwing up a few times on the cricket pitch but usually in the mornings after a night on the prowl. Nehra performed at the business end of a match watched by billions of people all over the world. I would say take a bow but he was already curled up on the pitch. Great stuff.

Coffin

In cricket terms your coffin is the big rectangular box you lug your gear around in and it is amazing what some players can fit in theirs. Ghetto blasters, five or six bats, gloves, pads, helmets, books, CDs, dirty mags and the odd bottle of the strong stuff all find their way into the boxes which must be much bigger on the inside than they are on the outside, like the Tardis in 'Dr Who.'

But there have been a few occasions when I've thought I would be going home in a wooden box instead of carrying one. On my first trip to Australia Craig McDermott asked me if I liked hospital food after he had a good look at one of the more spiteful wickets we played on that year. My nifty footwork kept my teeth in my mouth although I don't know if the square leg umpire enjoyed having me on his lap for the short time I was batting. More than one captain has threatened to strangle me but somehow I have escaped the dreaded box for now. Thank God cats get nine lives.

Collapse

If you have been in as many cricket dressing rooms as I have you will know when a collapse is coming on. Everything can be tickety-boo at 100-odd for zip when all the blokes who are paid to bat forget which end of the thing to hold. All of a sudden you're 120 for six and the tailenders are scrabbling around trying to remember where they put their pads.

For the bowlers this is a golden chance to score a few points off the top order. If you get a first-baller then you can explain quite reasonably that the bowling was lightning and if the boys going in first can't lay a bat on it how can you be expected to? After all the only time they bowl left-arm spin is when they are pissing around in the nets or at someone's benefit game when they are bowling to the chairman of selectors and their tour place is looking a bit iffy.

If your luck's in and you can nick 30 or so runs or even hang around for an hour or so you will gain the grudging admiration of the batters and the chance to call yourself an allrounder in the pub afterwards. And maybe push for a move up the order to number ten. Sod's Law says you will be back at number 11 one game later but it is worth it to see their faces when you come back in and chirp, "That bloke McGrath's not got much pace. What was the problem lads?" Even better if you've got the runs with a collection of Chinese cuts and thick outside edges — that will annoy them even more. It's not how, it's how many — right boys?

Compton

Nick Compton has got quite a lot to live up to, as have fellow Middlesex youngsters Mali 'son of Sir Viv' Richards and Ben 'grandson of Sir Len' Hutton.

Nick's granddad Denis was a legend at the club and played footie for the Gunners as well. He learnt his cricket in South Africa and, you read it here first, could well be the next Jacques Kallis.

Embers did a great job keeping news of Nick's contract quiet because he was still at school and was trying to concentrate on his A-levels. When the world famous football referee David Elleray, a teacher at Harrow, blew the whistle to the press that we were going to sign him, old Embers went ballistic. Obviously he has a lot to live up to with a name like his but he's got talent and I don't think you'll find him turning up for games in his dinner jacket like Denis used to.

Corridor Of Uncertainty

The corridor of uncertainty is an imaginary area found in the minds of coaches and one famous ex-Yorkshire opening batsman. It is definitely not in the vocabulary of Richards, Lara or Tendulkar.

The corridor is two imaginary lines just outside off stump and if the ball lands in this holy area the batsman can't decide whether to nick you to slip or play on. Geoff Boycott loves it and bangs on about it, but really it's just bowling a good line for a quick bowler. The Aussies reckon Glenn McGrath can put the ball in the corridor with a blindfold on and when he joined Worcester he walked straight off the plane and into the nets before bowling in the corridor for two hours. The whole point is to get the batsman caught in two minds whether to play the ball or leave it.

I think Micky Stewart invented the phrase on the 1989-90 tour of the West Indies. His way of countering a batting line-up that read Greenidge, Haynes, Richardson, Best, Hooper, Richards and Dujon was to bowl in the 'corridor,' Most of the time these batsmen are only uncertain whether to smash you through extra cover for six or over mid-off for a maximum. But to be fair to Stewart it did work on that tour. Especially in the first Test when a bloke called Fraser, leading an allegedly 'pop-gun' attack, got five-for by sticking rigidly to bowling in the corridor. Even Viv didn't know what to make of it. A sign of things to come for the big man who made a living out of bowling in the channel.

Corruption

When I heard that someone called Condon was going to be involved in cricket I thought he would be telling the boys about birth control rather than investigating a bit of palm-greasing.

Sir Paul Condon and his boys went round the world gathering evidence on the match-fixing stink and have not come up publicly with too much we didn't know already. However seeing as cricketers are so fond of their stats wouldn't it be easiest just to say that anyone who is caught with their fingers in the till gets all their records wiped out of *Wisden*? That way their whole careers would go down the swanny for the sake of a few quid.

County Cricket

Splitting the County Championship into two divisions has certainly livened up the end of the season and there are hardly any dead games now because virtually everyone is involved in some sort of promotion-relegation battle. My last season of county cricket was livened up no end by the tussle Middlesex were having to go up. The higher intensity is better for everyone — spectators and players — but it plays havoc with your social life.

If you have been knocking up some bit of crumpet in Leeds for one weekend a year for the past few seasons then I'm afraid your nooky is out of the window if the Yorkies get relegated.

Likewise with promotion. If you've been having an annual five-day fling with the landlady of some moody bed and breakfast in Cardiff then that particular dish is off the menu if you go up and the Welsh boyos don't produce the goods.

So is it any wonder county pros look so confused at the finish of some of these tight end-of-season games? If you have cultivated a relationship like that for a few years it only takes a couple of long-hops and all that hard work is out of the window and you're not even off the mark for next year. I don't know about brown envelopes full of cash but if anything is going to get your average pro to send down a few friendly half-volleys it is the thought of a guaranteed bunk-up with no strings attached.

Croft

The tubby turner always claims that playing for Glamorgan is like playing rugby for Wales and rolling out for England is like being in the British Lions. Well, I thought he was auditioning for the role of Lions' enforcer-in-chief when I saw him square up to Mark Illott at the end of a fiery one-day match between the Taffs and Essex.

In the end it was a case of handbags at ten paces but for a moment I thought it would really kick off. If Crofty had punched his weight then Mike Tyson would be trouble let alone the lanky Illott. He has got guts, though, as he showed when holding out the South Africans at Old Trafford for 37 not out and keeping us in a series we were to go on and win. Unfortunately nought for 100-odd meant he was left out of the side for the next game. He took it on the chin, though, and apparently was the first on the phone when the series was won at Headingley.

Once though the crafty Taff ruined one of the most promising innings of my career. Middlesex were deep in the crapper against Glamorgan at Sophia Gardens when Justin Langer decided to go crazy and make an unbeaten 213. The highlight of this magnificent knock was a last wicket partnership of 56 with yours truly of which Justin scored 55 and leg byes managed one.

Crofty took nearly an hour to work out that I was the weaker of the two players at the wicket despite the immaculate forward defensive I had been playing and ruthlessly targeted me with some vicious off-spin. I would like to report that the ball spat from a length before rapping me on the glove, but I'm afraid I was beaten in the flight and lobbed a return catch to my old sparring partner just as I'd got my eye in and another promising knock was cut short. Always the way.

Curtly and Courtney

Off the pitch two of the friendliest lads you could hope to meet and Curtly Ambrose is a bit of a wizard on the bass with his band after games. But put a piece of red leather into their outsize mitts and they turn into wide-eyed maniacs. They were so popular in their homeland that groundsmen fell over backwards to prepare pitches that satisfied their bloodlust.

The first time I toured the West Indies with England in 1994 I was lucky enough to be left out of the side which played in Trinidad and watched the goings on with the morbid fascination of a spectator at a public execution. Except it was my mates who were having their heads chopped off.

We needed 190 odd to win and the travelling fans plus a big gang of sailors from HMS Newcastle thought we would walk it. So did I until Athers trudged back into the dressing room after a first baller from Curts. Then it was a procession and I felt like that reporter in the Falklands who "counted them all out and counted them back" — in very quick succession.

In non-Curtly circumstances the next two batsmen in would be padded up, but that day in Trinidad the last FIVE were sitting in a row with their helmets on looking like a bunch of parachutists waiting for a tap on the shoulder before they leapt to their deaths.

On a billiard table Curtly would be hard to play but on a fizzing Trinidadian greentop in front of a leaping crowd he was just about impossible. Even Stewie and Judge who actually like playing the quicks could not handle him in that mood.

People often ask me for batting tips and how I prepare mentally when I'm about to go out to face the pace merchants. I have a well rehearsed routine which involves fags and long periods in the little boys' room — you know the sort of thing. The best place to play these lads from is a nice deckchair on the balcony with a cup of tea in your hand.

God knows how Courtney Walsh kept going so long and after Amby retired he carried the Windies attack on his own. He did not cherrypick which games to play in for Gloucestershire or the West Indies — he gave pros a bad name, not a niggly groin in sight when he didn't fancy a Sunday League match.

He did not pound the ground like some grunt and groan quicks I could name. You could hardly hear him come up to the wicket which was probably just as well. It did not matter whether you batted one or 11 he treated all batsmen with the same loathing. The treatment he dished out to Athers in Jamaica made me feel sick just watching it from the safety of the pavilion.

Cut

The worst shot in the book if you are spinner. To be cut is the cardinal sin in slow bowling circles because even if the ball turns the batsman has got plenty of time to adjust before smashing you to the boundary. A good player of spin will try and disrupt your length with a bit of fancy footwork but you can't afford to be fooled even if he is performing a Come Dancing routine down the other end. As soon as you've released the cherry he will rock back and knock the cover off the ball. Drop short at my pace and you're history.

Warnie could get away with it if he bowled his top-spinner a bit short and it hurried onto the batsman's pads but he's different from the rest of us.

Is For ...
Daffy
Daisy Cutter
Dessie
Devil's Number
Discipline
Divorce
Down His Throat
Dress Code
Drinking
Drinks Waiter
Driving
Drugs
Duck
Duckworth Lewis

Daffy

Phil DeFreitas was an old mate of mine from our days as kids at Lord's and inspired me to take cricket really seriously when he got in Gatt's Ashes tour party and brought back the spoils.

He was another player to be saddled with being the Next Botham especially after the man himself took Daffy under his wing on that triumphant trip. Still, with 44 Tests to his name he did better than most of the pretenders and is one of a very elite band of bowlers to have taken over 1,000 first class wickets. I wonder who else has done that?!

I thought we were going to get a touch of the Bothams when he was batting in the 1987 World Cup final and England were dead and buried. Suddenly my old mucker started laying into Craig McDermott, hitting him for a massive six and two fours in the 47th over. Game on. He had to go for his shots so there was no disgrace in holing out but if he had pulled that off he could have asked for and got the freedom of St John's Wood. As it was it motivated a scrawny left-arm spinner to get his arse in gear and go for it.

Daisy Cutter

A deadly delivery but not one you can bowl at will. You have to rely on the groundsman to produce a dodgy track if you're going to see one, and as most of them are susceptible to a pint of the brown stuff you should always have seen a few by the third day of a championship game. The ball rolls along the floor after pitching and hits the batsman dead in front or bowls him because he can't get his bat down in time. Beautiful when it happens but the batsmen always go dolly when they are on the receiving end.

On the 1998 tour to the Windies, Nasser Hussain attracted daisy cutters, or shooters as they are sometimes called, like a free bar attracts the Barmy Army. I am afraid to say that on one or two occasions he let himself become a little temperamental and the dressing room furniture got the benefit of his blade.

Whenever batsmen are out like this they forget all the

times the've had the benefit of the doubt with moody LBW decisions or nicking the ball to the keeper and not walking and lose it completely. Bats fly, windows are put through and doors ripped off their hinges. Keep the jibes about it being a batsman's game and it all evening out over the season to yourself or you could end up with a Gray Nicholls long handle up your tradesman's entrance.

Dessie

Not the great racehorse but a different type of thoroughbred. The West Indian batsman Des Haynes belonged to the Caribbean school of batting which believed bowlers should be able to hurl down six bouncers an over so he could hook them out of the ground. Just because he could play the short stuff he thought everyone else enjoyed playing it as well.

He would goad the Middlesex quicks when he was fielding at short leg by calling out "He wants it on the top floor Gussie, you're bowling in the basement."

When he was batting he would encourage the opposition pace men to bounce him out. He once banged on the Northants dressing room door after we had won the toss and told Curtly Ambrose he was going to hook him out of sight. Curtly naturally tested him out and true to his word Des hooked him out of the ground. Frightening stuff.

That's all very well if you can bat like Des but the rest of us thought he was off his trolley. And once he had had his fun it was down to the rest of the batters to confront a thoroughly pissed off Mr Ambrose.

Devil's Number

Some of my ex's might say the devil's number will put you straight through to my mobile but it is an Aussie term used to describe 87. When an Australian batsman gets to 87, (13 away from a ton — geddit?) he is immediately supposed to start crapping himself in case the jinx strikes and he gets out.

Apparently the old allrounder Keith Miller had seen Don Bradman fail by getting out for a mere 87 when he was a kid and thought the figure must be capable of some kind of black magic. In those days if Bradman didn't get into the mid-250s he had screwed up. According to the books far more Aussie bats get out for the other scores in the 80s so it looks like a load more cobblers from down under. I never had the chance to test out the magic number, but I'm sure I'll get there in a charity match, probably facing the hostile bowling of someone like Mick Jagger or Nicholas Parsons, before too long.

Discipline

Coaches and ex-majors from the home counties are always banging on about discipline and I have been on the wrong end of more than a few fines for my performances on and off the field. On tours you can be fined for anything from kicking your hat to wearing the wrong shirt to a function so you have to build those into your budget.

But some of the disciplinary procedures have got out of hand. In 2002 I was the second player to be reprimanded under a new code of conduct — the first was English cricket's other awkward customer Andy Caddick.

My crime was to use inappropriate language in a match at Lord's against Durham. I would like to know what is appropriate language when it is 95 degrees, the wicket is like a road and the opposition are in the process of piling up 645. "Sorry old chap, shall I serve you up another couple of half-volleys so you can get your double hundred a bit quicker"? Tempers are bound to fray a bit in professional sport and it is not as if the umpires are miked up yet like the referees in rugby so maybe we should leave what happens in the heat of the moment out on the paddock.

Similarly, a couple of years before that I was in hot water for, as the tabloids like to put it, "clashing with Essex's Ian Flanagan." I'd had a decent shout for a bat-pad catch turned down and allegedly blocked him next ball when he was going for a single. Not guilty M'Lud, I was just walking casually back to my mark by the most direct route.

Once I even managed to get hit in the pocket for throwing the ball in a quote 'aggressive manner,' I was in Australia at the time where you spend as much time ducking throws from fielders as you do ducking bouncers. Anyway, if I had meant to hit the batsman I'm sure I could have managed it from that short range.

Cricket is a passionate game and if you don't get steamed up about it what's the point in playing? People have claimed my attitude has been wrong in the past and if it is wrong to want to win desperately then I have been out of line. In other countries they applaud people who are hard on themselves and on the opposition. The Aussie batsman Ricky Ponting was fuming against West Indies early in 2003 when he was out stumped in Trinidad — and he was on 206 at the time.

If you chuck in the number of times I've had my match fee slashed because of some minor altercation with a player (on one side or another), an umpire or some blazer then I've taken some big financial hits in my career — due to my 'indiscipline,'

Off the pitch if a bloke sees you in the boozer having a casual half of lager, the next day in the papers you have had a fight with the barman and been dancing naked on the tables. All because someone in there has seen your face on the telly and you will be hit in the pocket once more.

Tack on a couple of divorces and it's no wonder I'm still filling in my lottery tickets every Saturday night.

Divorce

Divorce will be my specialist subject in the unlikely event that I get invited onto 'Mastermind' after seeing the proceeds of a decent benefit year go up in smoke recently and head their way towards the former Mrs Tufnell.

It is a wonder any marriage in Test cricket lasts more than a couple of years. No other sport makes such demands on a relationship and in terms of money they won't be making a sequel to 'Footballers' Wives' about England cricketers and their other halves. If you are lucky enough to play for England you can be away for four months every winter and then when you get home it is back to the county circuit where you spend more time in strange beds than in your own. I am not the only one of my era to have problems in the marriage department, most of the lads go through dodgy patches.

The wives do get out for some of the more glamorous bits of overseas tours and let's face it Melbourne is not a bad place to spend Christmas if you are used to London's Archway, and Barbados in March is not too shabby either.

But in my experience if you are on tour on your own then the missus thinks, "The Cat's away and he's at play." And she would only be half wrong. And because the papers follow you around everywhere on every England trip you can guarantee that your dalliance with a local lap dancer will hit the front page of the tabloids if you are married. If you're single on tour you can shag everything in sight and no one gives a toss.

Down His Throat

Every time a batsman is caught in the deep the commentators claim it went straight down your throat, neglecting the time you spent circling underneath the ball waiting for it to arrive back on Planet Earth. Since giving up the game its only relevance to me is what gets poured down my throat, usually from large bottles.

Dress Code

Trying to keep up with the dress regulations on an England tour is like painting the Forth Bridge or chasing a cover drive from Adam Gilchrist — you can never catch up. An English cricketer abroad will have at least five sets of clothes that must be worn at certain times.

You've got your whites for playing and some pyjamas for the hit-and-giggle stuff. Plus two sets of training gear. One casual when the game is on and you're posing for the birds in the crowd on the balcony and one for the nets. Then you have the number ones for official hobnobbing bashes at the ambassador's house plus some ultra fashionable 'smart but casual' stuff — usually grey slacks and polo shirts (a big hit with the ladies).

It beats the hell out of me and my wallet. If you wear the wrong stuff at the wrong time you get hit in the pocket. Try explaining to the missus that she can't have a new washing machine because you wore the wrong strides at a photocall. When I got back from the West Indies in 1998 I barely had enough of my tour fee left for the cab ride home from Heathrow airport. Three months away working non-stop and I was virtually skint (I will hold my hands up to a fairly hefty bar bill which could have had something to do with it). That was a definite no to the new washing machine the then Mrs Tufnell had set her heart on.

On my next trip the new coach Duncan Fletcher had obviously not done his background research on me. Unbelievably I was put on the management committee of senior players with Athers, Butch and Goughie to rule on squad complaints, tour rules and, of all things, dress codes. Players could come to us if they had problems and we would then go to the management and try to sort it out. Me, Philip Charles Roderick Tufnell, a respected senior pro, a member of the hierachy and a shoulder to cry on. With my reputation?

Drinking

I have never kept a log book of the number of beers I have poured down my throat but my admiration for the unnamed Test bowler who said the year after his international debut that his ambition was to drink 1,000 pints by the end of the season is boundless. Imagine challenging yourself like that. I am told he had hit the landmark by July and by the end of the season he had more than 1,500 to his name. The fact that he managed to play for England again after getting all that down his neck makes him a legend in this neck of the woods.

Drinks Waiter

The worst job on tour is to be the drinks waiter for the lads when you've not been picked in the starting line-up for a match. You fancy a rest at some stage on most trips and a couple of days R&R on a secluded beach with a vat of rum punch and a bit of local crumpet can perk up even the most jaded tourist. So when you get told to go to the ground to be 12th man it goes down like the proverbial lead balloon.

The 12th man is just a glorified skivvy. You don't just take a tray of orange squash out at every drinks interval you just never get the chance to sit down. Batsmen will want new gloves, bats and helmets plus extra drinks if it is a hot one — which it always is on tour and that's why you wanted to go down to the beach in the first place. You have to look after their every need. Like making sure they get the messages on their mobiles without their other halves intercepting them and shouting the racing results out when they are in the middle.

The batsmen love having you running around pandering to them, bringing them fresh gloves while they knock some part-time bowling around to give their figures a boost.

Driving

When I was a young pro at Middlesex I used to get some funny looks from the blokes on the gate when I parked my Porsche in the car park. Well despite more than 18 years in the game I never managed to upgrade it. In fact in my last season I was driving round an old heap that was more like a skip than a car. There are a few lawyers driving round in Porsches now thanks to me though.

Drugs

The first time I encountered drugs in cricket was on the 46 all out tour to the Caribbean with England. The crowd at Sabina Park in Jamaica is pretty laid back most of the time and after fielding at fine leg for a couple of hours in a one-day international I knew why. I'd smelt funny fags before but the stuff the punters were smoking must have been high grade wacky backy.

Clouds of aromatic smoke were drifting past me as the crowd puffed away and I was left feeling a bit light-headed. In fact by the time Des Haynes had unleashed a few tracer bullets to the fence I was completely wasted. My eyes were on stalks and I could hardly put one foot in front of the other. I felt like I was going to pass out and when the skipper signalled that I was going to come on to bowl I wish I'd fainted there and then.

Athers asked me to loosen up but he needn't have bothered. I was so loose my legs felt like they were made out of rubber and my usual chirpy hop, skip and a jump approach to the wicket was more of a crawl than a run-up.

The skipper did not get to Cambridge University by being dim so he knew that I was in no fit state to bowl and after four overs of dross had disappeared he swiftly took me off and made me field in close. Cheers. You try stopping a cover drive going at full tilt if you can see four balls coming at you.

Duck

Batsmen are a superstitious lot and never eat duck the night before going out to bat. I've never gone along with that. I used to eat whatever I fancied unfortunately it never helped me get off the mark.

Duckworth Lewis

I might not want to spend a night in the boozer with Frank Duckworth and Tony Lewis but somehow this pair of boffins have made the best fist of sorting out rain-affected one-day games.

Apparently Mr Duckworth is the editor of something called the Royal Statistical Society's Monthly Newsletter — a rag that has passed me by as someone obviously forgot to stick my subscription in the post.

Like all pros, I have memorised the sheets of tables that explain the details of the Duckworth Lewis method but I'll keep it simple. Basically the more wickets you have lost if you are chasing the more runs you have to get because you have got less 'resources' left.

Targets are also adjusted by when in the innings the rain comes and runs, wickets and overs are all taken into account. For instance if a side only has 30 overs to bat they will give it a bit more welly than if they had their full 50 so their total has to be adjusted in the eyes of Messrs Duckworth and Lewis. Fair enough I say. Although I have seen some games where a side scoring more runs in less overs than the opposition has lost. And some games have finished with the players on the pitch not having a clue who has won so God knows what the crowd think.

It might look like your worst school nightmare but the

method is better than anything anyone else has come up with.

In the 1992 World Cup in Australia the 'rain rule' threatened to ruin the whole competition. It was something to do with the overs you scored least off being scrubbed if there was a bit of rain that shortened the opposition's innings. It sounded great in theory until we got to the semi-final against South Africa. They needed 22 off 13 balls when the heavens opened and when they came back on the pitch they needed 22 from one Chris Lewis delivery. To be honest I think the boys were a bit embarrassed about it. Even Chris Lewis, on one of his 'enigmatic days' could not manage to bowl enough no-balls to give them a chance. Although justice was done and we got into the final, the method was rightly scrapped with the lovechild of Duckworth and Lewis coming in some time in 1997.

So if there is rain in the air you'll often see English batsmen bringing out scraps out of paper with D-L charts on so they can pace their innings properly. I expect some of the youngsters with big muscles will soon have the charts tattooed onto their forearms.

After all the problems the Springboks have had over the years with rain you would have thought they would have the charts on them in the 2003 tournament. I know the economy is a bit wobbly down there but you would have thought they could have stretched to a few bits of photocopying. Obviously not and in a tournament which had a few farcical moments the way the hosts went out was right up there with the best.

The Sri Lankans racked up 268 and had the Boks 229 for six with five overs left before it started pissing down and all bets were off. According to our old pals D-L the game was a tie and the teams shared the points forcing the hosts to leave their own party before the beer had been brought out. At the time Mark Boucher was going great guns, had just smashed a six and punched the air as if the job was done. Not quite. A cheeky single would have left his side in the tournament and the keeper with a life's supply of Castle Lager but he just blocked it and blew it. Somehow nobody had checked the charts properly, but the Sri Lankans claimed they knew what was going on all along, and the South Africans were scuppered.

Is For ...
Earrings
ECB
Edmonds
Elephants
Eleven
Embers
Endorsements
Essex
Extra Cover

Earrings

Some of the West Indian boys wear more jewellery than Mr T in the 'A Team' and when they run into bowl you can hear the jangling before they come into view. But the dangers of wearing the stuff became clear when Ramnaresh Sarwan was crusted by the Sri Lankan bowler Dilhara Fernando in the last World Cup. Now Fernando's a decent bowler but Andy Roberts he ain't so I was shocked to see the blood streaming from Sarwan's head as if someone had hit him on the side of the head with a tomahawk. Fortunately it was not the work of a mad axe-man. The ball had hit him flush on a rather lovely gold stud which went into the side of his head leaving him covered in claret and in need of a stitch-up job in the local casualty department. I don't think he will be wearing it again just as my earring did not last long once I became a pro cricketer.

My own earring went shortly after I started at Lord's. Derek Pringle got enough stick when he turned up to play for England sporting a hoop in his lug-hole and he had been to university. Sometimes you have just got to play the game and I thought it best to cut my losses and discard it. I would have loved to have played cricket as if I was the lead singer of Oasis, with stubble, dangly earrings and a beer in my hand but you just have to bite the bullet and be a good boy occasionally.

Darren Gough went the other way when he appeared late in his career sporting a diamond stud that would not have looked out of place on Jennifer Lopez at the Oscars. Those quick bowlers must be on better money than spinners as these days I couldn't afford a curtain ring.

ECB

There was no danger of my offshore bank account ever being swollen by a central contract so I never felt as if I had to toe the party line with regards to the people who claim they run the game. Now I've called it quits I am still convinced they are among the most bone-headed bunch ever to be put in charge of a national game.

When the England and Wales Cricket Board was formed after

the Test and County Cricket Board was disbanded in 1997 it promised radical change in the game in England. A lot of the same faceless faces seem to be in the jobs they had before but to be fair they have achieved one or two minor victories.

England players on tour now get a room to themselves, a good thing if you have ever prepared for an Ashes Test abroad by listening to Wayne Larkins open beer cans or watching Jack Russell washing his smalls in the hotel bathroom. That's down to Ian MacLaurin who was shocked to see the hovels we were sleeping in one tour while the bigwigs were living it up in a posh hotel down the road.

The split in the county championship is definitely a good thing, promoting more competitive cricket at the arse-end of the season and the academy should start to pay dividends in the next couple of seasons.

However, all the good they have done was wiped out in one hit when the Zimbabwe affair erupted. The whole thing was the biggest shambles ever in a sport that knows a thing or two about administrative cock-ups and after the World Cup it got even worse.

Work this one out. After the will-they, won't-they saga the penny-pinching ECB got worried that the Zimbos would not turn up to play a couple of Tests in England.

So what does David Morgan, who had been in the job five minutes, do? He only agrees on behalf of the team to go to Zimbabwe in 2004 as long as they fulfil their fixtures over here. The England football team managed to cancel going to Zimbabwe for a training camp when they went to South Africa but we still have to go over there and play a couple of Tests. Unbelievable.

Everyone knew what was going on in Zimbabwe but because our board are worried about losing the dosh from two Test matches they agree to go back over there and support the dictatorship of Robert Mugabe. So once the World Cup was over and nothing had changed they agree to jump into bed with Mugabe. What message does that send to Henry Olonga, who at the time was in hiding after receiving death threats over his black armband protest? It says come over here

Henry and we will crap on everything you have stood for. I am surprised Mr Olonga came over here at all. He must be a forgiving sort of a bloke.

So at the same time as we were spending billions and risking soldiers' lives to try and overthrow one tyrant in the Middle East we were arranging to play cricket in another one's back garden. Why not invite him over for tea in the pavilion on the first day of the Lord's Test match as well and have done with it. Even by the ECB's standards this one was priceless.

What happens to a player who says he is not going to tour Zimbo because he doesn't think he will be safe or he doesn't happen to agree with the way that Mugabe treats the people over there? Will he be told to shut it and get on the plane or will his career be cut short? Or will he have to go and worry about stepping over dead bodies as he gets off the bus and goes into the ground?

Edmonds

When I arrived at Middlesex I could not work out Phil Edmonds. He was obviously a good bowler but he was constantly thinking about things outside cricket. I was slightly in awe of the strokes he used to pull as well. You would not have taken short odds about him eventually becoming chairman of Middlesex then, but chairman he is, proving there is a place for eccentric left arm spinners running the English game.

He had a good turn of phrase and some of the one-liners he came out with would have done a stand-up comedian proud. When he came back from India once someone asked him what he was looking forward to most and he replied, "a dry fart." Having been there on a very long tour, and experienced more than my fair share of the non-cricketing runs, I know exactly what he meant.

He had some sort of property business which he seemed to do very well out of because you couldn't hit the business end of a wine list in those days like he could on a county cricketer's salary. When everyone else in the side was obsessed by winning the county championship he seemed to have something more important on his mind. And he didn't always see eye to eye with Gatt. Apparently he got bored with the grind of the county circuit and used to go home when Middlesex were batting, telling the boys to give him a ring if we lost a couple of wickets and it looked like he would be needed in the middle. I must admit I liked his style.

When I was still in the stiffs, the first team had a game against Sussex and when the story of 'Henri's' performance got back I thought that was the last we would see of him on this earth let alone in the Middlesex side.

Apparently Gatt and Henri had a barney about the field placings and when Middlesex batted they were holding out for a draw. Obviously at times like this the self-respecting tailender does his best to look like he is getting into line with the ball just in case the skipper is watching and makes out that he is doing his best to keep the bowling out.

But Henri had different ideas. He lasted four balls — dancing up the wicket and slog-sweeping before he was bowled. When the spinner returned to the dressing room with a smirk on his face and told his captain he might as well fine him there and then Gatt's face apparently was darker than the Burgundy Edmonds used to drink. Gatt went ballistic but knew Edmonds was too good to get rid of. Little did he know that Edmonds' eventual left-arm replacement would cause him a lot more grief.

Elephants

I copped a bit of flak after my first visit to India when I ruined a future career in the diplomatic corps with the elephants reference but the truth is I had never seen anything like it in my life. In 1993 I was not enjoying myself on tour and not pulling up any trees on the pitch so my "done the elephants, done the poverty, might as well go home" quote did not go down too well with the locals or the tour management who were trying to keep up everyone's spirits when we were being tonked by the Indians.

Highgate Hill does not prepare you for Bombay High Street and I could not take it all in. As soon as you left the hotel you got hit by a wall of noise that did not stop until you got back at night. The only relief you got was when you shut your hotel windows and put the telly on full blast for the latest Bollywood classic. Driving to the game was like something out of the Wacky Races without Penelope Pitstop, but with plenty of Dick Dastardlies and Mutleys.

India is not normally a happy hunting ground for visiting spinners — in fact it's a bloody graveyard. Even Warnie has struggled there so what hope is there for the rest of us?

The home batsmen do not wake up screaming in the middle of the night if they have got to face slow bowling on one of their pitches the next morning. Robin Smith was fielding close in during one game and ran up to tell me that he could see fear in the eyes of the Indian batsmen as they prepared to face me. That was just Judge being positive. When they ran past me I had a look in their eyes for this doomed expression and I couldn't see any of it.

To make matters worse they are used to performing in front of 100,000 screaming lunatics.

Playing in Calcutta is like playing in a washing machine. Noise, banks of people moving up and down and the stands on the point of collapse. Oh, and they let them light bonfires in the stand as well so it is a million miles away from playing at Southgate where the only things that get lit in the ground have beefburgers on top of them or come out of a pack of 20.

Then into this mayhem walks Mister Sachin Tendulkar. If Lara is a prince in Trinidad, this bloke is a god in India. The attention he gets from the fans and the media makes David Beckham look like a pub player on Hackney Marshes. He whacks your first two balls for four and all of a sudden the crowd are going absolutely ballistic, you don't know where to pitch the ball and you've got to bowl four more of the bastards. That is when you realise you are playing a different game from the one back home.

On top of all that you also have to contend with dodgy guts (see Bob's Bistro). In 1993 every member of the tour party went down with a dose of Gandhi's revenge and the smog, which was so thick that Ted Dexter announced plans for a scientific study on the pollution. I may have had a few fags on the trip but the fact that you couldn't see past your hand was not down to me. Even our scorer had to fly home and Dermot Reeve's mum stepped in and did a stint of book duty.

To acclimatise us for the heat, dust and general lack of air we were sent to Lilleshall. That's right. To prepare for three months in blistering heat on the subcontinent we were sent to deepest Shropshire in December. It's no surprise that some of us did not do the business on the pitch — we would have been better off having nets in a gas chamber — that would have got us used to not being able to breath. It's hard enough bowling spin at Indian batsmen as it is without having to do it with a gas mask on and a cork up your arse.

Eleven

My lucky number.

Embers

John Emburey and I had a good thing going at Middlesex as players before he jumped ship and went to Northampton. But it was good to have him back at HQ as coach before I called time on my county career.

He was a real thinker, never afraid to give his opinion or advice and definitely not scared of bowling on good wickets. He also believed in giving tutorials to young left arm spinners in the nearest boozer to the ground.

Ernie would take one look at a belting batting strip and declare, "If you don't win the toss on this Gatt we are fecked." Of course, Gatt would call wrongly and after the quicks had given up on bowling on such a good deck Embers would be on by 12 o'clock. He would then twirl away for hours and end up with three for 65 from about 35 overs. Captains kill for that sort of control.

He even threatened to get his bowling boots back on when I left and there is no doubt that he could still do a good holding job. You can't buy the experience he has got.

When I was on at the other end he would be standing at slip and I always wanted to impress him. I was a young kid and he had been there done it and won the Ashes — not many people still involved in the game have that sort of scalp on their mantelpiece. He hammered home to me that you must bowl to a plan and he had something up his sleeve for every batsman on the circuit, which was logged into his memory bank. Even if it was nothing more earth shattering than a way to keep them quiet for a bit.

He used to take me to the pub and reveal the cunning schemes he had for me to get Viv Richards out when we played Glamorgan and although they didn't always work there was always a bit of logic behind them. His batting style was unique though and I think one of the commentators invented the word 'nurdle' for some of his shots. But he averaged over 20 in the first class game and scored a few hundreds. People in glass houses and all that...

Endorsements

Like everything else in cricket, batsmen dominate the sponsorship department although a few bat companies slipped me a few quid not to use their products. The batsmen have so many bits of kit that they are in the money if they get half of it sponsored. They could nick 30 grand a year in sponsorship while me and Gus struggled by on a two and sixpence boot deal.

Bowlers have their boots and unless you get the soles sponsored and do a swallow dive when you deliver the ball your chances of earning a bit of extra cash are pretty non-existent. Gus, who could at least hold a bat without dropping it, struggled in vain to get a decent deal for years so instead of going out with a plain plank he started putting his own designs on them.

Once upon a time you could only have stickers from bat manufacturers on your blade but once that rule was overturned some of the blades you saw out in the middle looked more like an advertising board than something to punish bowlers with. A couple of the weightier chaps got money from restaurants or fast food joints which got me thinking. I thought some of the curry houses of north London would have jumped at the chance to have their name on my bat but the call never came.

Essex

Apart from that lot with the brown caps from south of the river, Essex are Middlesex's biggest rivals and games against them are always pretty spiky.

Ronnie Irani, the Essex skipper, is one of my biggest mates in cricket and is a regular companion on trips to some of the more salubrious night-spots in the capital. As you would expect from a bloke like Ronnie he showed a touch of class at Southgate in 2002. Both sides were pushing for promotion so obviously we were not going to let them take any liberties. They wanted us to declare our second innings and set up a run chase on the final day but our skipper Andrew Strauss, with the top of the table as tight as a gnat's arse, was having none of it.

The Essex boys all got the hump until Ronnie injected a bit of humour into proceedings by ordering the 12th man to bring the fielders ice-creams at the drinks break. He wandered onto the pitch carrying a box filled with, according to the paper the next day, seven strawberry ices, four cornettos and one choc ice — but nothing for our batsmen.

The fielders then sat down on the edge of the square and ate their ice-creams as if they were at a picnic. Any Australian walking past would have thought the world had gone mad.

At least at the end of the season both teams got promoted. I would never have forgiven Straussie if our go-slow had meant an end to our nights out in Chelmsford. As it turned out my love affair with the place ended just as the boys were playing a pre-season friendly in the snow the following spring.

Extra Cover

To be taken out before boarding the plane to the West Indies if you can find a gullible insurance rep. It's also a fielding position for the most agile player on the park. I am told.

Is For ...
Fags
Fancy Dress
Fashanu
Featherbed
Fielding
Filth
Fine Leg
Fitness
Fletcher, D
Fletcher, K
Flintoff
Freemantle Doctor
Full Bung

Fags

I had the Oasis song 'Cigarettes and Alcohol' to walk out to during my brief flirtation with one-day international cricket and because of that seemed to have been labelled, along with Warnie, as the only player who likes a chuff in these health conscious days. Funny how there are so many secret smokers in the dressing room and we're the only ones who get fingered by the papers. They should go into the bogs when wickets are tumbling. All the traps are occupied and it looks like a scene out of an old Sherlock Holmes movie with white clouds everywhere.

When the ECB were questioned about their attitude to smoking a few years ago they said that a Test match was a high pressure environment and was mentally draining. They also said that if we wanted to have a smoke in the dressing room at the end of such a tough game then that was fair enough. Quite.

Don't forget what Mark Butcher did at Headingley against the Aussies. If it wasn't quite Botham's Ashes, Butch did a pretty good impression of Beefy 20 years after his famous game in 1981. Chasing over 300 to win Butch weighed in with 173 not out and announced that during the lunch break he had sat in the shower with a couple of gaspers and a cup of coffee. Not a salad in sight. I don't think it was a coincidence that the selectors recalled the most notorious smoker in the game for the next Test at The Oval. Unfortunately my unique methods of preparation did not pay dividends that time.

Fancy Dress

People might say I spent 18 years in fancy dress being dressed up as a cricketer but being a dab hand with the scissors and cotton is invaluable on tour. When we were away on tours we used to have a fancy dress party on Christmas Day with the press boys. (Except the time it got cancelled when relations between us and the scribblers hit an all-time low).

In Australia Gatt didn't need much dressing up to do a decent impression of Henry the Eighth while Daffy looked great as Batman and Hicky flexed his muscles in a Fred Flintstone outfit. I did my best Elvis impression and one of the boys, who shall remain nameless, dressed as a Fairy Queen. I was a bit surprised to see that he had grown quite attached to his silky underwear and was still wearing it a week later when we were getting changed for a Test match.

Fashanu

One of the most eye-popping things I saw in two weeks in the jungle was Fash the Bash, or John Fashanu as he is known in real-life, working his way through 1,000 sit-ups in one session.

I doubt if I've hit the four-figure mark in my career let alone in one sitting and yet there he was barely breaking sweat as he went through the milestone. After that he would spend about an hour on the punch bag knocking seven bells out of it before moving onto his next exercise. I have seem some fit cricketers in my time but even Goochie would have gone white if he had seen the stuff that Fash was getting up to.

When Fash was a footballer he played for Wimbledon, a group of lads who were nicknamed 'The Crazy Gang' for their antics, which involved all the old stuff, like underwear, Ralgex and fire extinguishers. He might have retired from the game a few years ago but he's obviously still one tinny short of a six-pack as they say down under.

Eels round his head, insects in his undies, rats, heights — he copped the lot in the trials in the jungle and gets a big pat on the back from yours truly. Apart from anything else he made pretty sure we didn't starve out there and his early morning stretching sessions are now a regular part of the Tufnell day. Not.

It was the first time in about 20 years that anyone has managed to get me properly warmed up without a few pints of pop inside me and that was a bit of an eye-opener I must admit. It's no wonder Fash survived all those trials — he is over 40 and still one of the fittest guys I've met in my life.

And a big lad as well. When he said "stretch" we stretched, don't worry about that. Philip Tufnell stretching his hamstrings at seven o'clock in the morning. Athers must have been pissing himself watching me do that.

Featherbed

To be honest I've always preferred playing on a waterbed than a featherbed. A featherbed is a flat pitch that does nothing for the bowlers except drive them mad. You don't mind slogging your guts out on a floating aquarium with a local lovely but on a featherbed you still get all the sweat but none of the rewards.

Fielding

The standard of fielding has improved out of all recognition since the days when opening bowlers wouldn't bend down to tie up their own bootlaces let alone field off someone else's bowling. Fielding has developed into a skill all of its own and for a man with my reputation I am ashamed to say that I played a small part in its development. Modesty prevents me from claiming all the credit for lifting fielding standards all around the world but I like to think I played a role.

Back in 1994 when I was still considered fit enough to be playing one-day internationals, I started the trend for sliding and athletically dragging the ball back before it hit the boundary rope. This wasn't the result of hard practice or even deep thought but was just to stop me fracturing my skull on the concrete barrier that surrounds Sabina Park.

In the second one-dayer of that tour to the Caribbean, Des Haynes pushed the ball past me at mid-on and as I sprawled on the ground I realised it would not have the legs to make it to the fence. So instead of a leisurely jog to the boundary edge and a slurp of a spectator's rum punch I had to get into international cricketer mode and sprint after the ball like it says in the job description. Oh bollocks.

Sprinting like a madman, I realised the concrete was rushing quickly towards me so I dived onto the deck and managed to scoop the ball back before it hit the rope and just avoided a frontal lobotomy. Gus was pissing himself but little did he know that because of my athleticism it would be written into all bowlers' contracts from that day on that they have to leap around in the outfield trying to turn a four into a three to make someone else's figures look good. No wonder he quit when he did.

But now it has gone too far. Look at poor old Simon Jones who nearly ended his career when he went sliding after a ball at Brisbane. In the summer he had looked the genuine article when he put the wind up the Indians at Lord's but because he has to slide around the pitch he busts his knee up and puts his whole livelihood at risk. You wouldn't have seen Fred Trueman getting his knees dirty or risking a slipped disc trying to save a couple of runs.

Some players, and you know who you are boys, think they have to slip round on their arses just to prove they are trying and to impress the skipper. If the opposition are 650-2 do you really think anyone notices the fact that it could have been 651-2 but for you risking a broken neck on an outfield full of potholes, broken bottles and pigeon shit?

If you're stationed on the longest boundary at the Melbourne Cricket Ground by some sadistic skipper you're better off kicking the ball over the boundary for four sometimes. The batsmen will only run five or six after your first pathetic throw from the fence has only made it halfway to the keeper. If you give the ball a sly nudge over the ropes everyone is too busy watching the replay on the big screen to see your feeble attempt at hurling the ball in over the stumps.

Having said all that, it is comforting as a bowler to have good fielders in the key positions like cover point where they can make the route to the boundary look a lot smaller than it is. David Gower and Derek Randall made fielding look glamorous when I started taking an interest in cricket but South Africa's Jonty Rhodes has been the best exponent of the art in recent times.

He was the engine room of the side when he was fielding and although his constant chirruping was a pain in the arse for the batting side, and the television audience, he kept everyone on their toes in the field. Even running to collect the bowlers' caps and giving them to the umpires — no one ever thought of saving my legs halfway through a marathon spell.

You might not like the way he wanted to dedicate the 2003 World Cup to the discredited Hansie Cronje but he used to put the shits up the batsmen when he was lurking at cover point. He was worth about 20 runs a game more than he ever scored with the bat. I wish I could have said the same.

Filth

Some of the magazines found in the average county player's grubby kitbag could certainly be described as filth but on the circuit filth refers to bowling that gets carted. Gus would bowl his one half-volley of the season then go all red-faced shouting "that's f****** filth Fraser."

Fine Leg

It is an insult to any keeper when the skipper tells you to move to very fine fine leg when he means he wants you to stand straight behind the iron-gloved stumper who has been missing balls all afternoon.

If you get asked to do this it is best to go to a normal fine leg and then creep behind the keeper while he is concentrating on the bowler. It is also a good place to leer at the fine pairs of legs walking around the ground.

Fitness

When I was a player a lot was made of my unique way of preparing for a game. Apparently you were better off having a sleepless night looking at your hotel walls than having a couple of beers to make sure you could get some kip. If you are a bit nervy the night before a game it is always best to unwind with a couple of cold ones.

To be honest it doesn't matter how you get ready for a match as long as you do the business on the pitch. In any sport who would you rather have walking out with you? Someone who can bench press three times his body weight or a bloke who will take a bullet (or a Brett Lee missile) for you in the chest.

You were more likely to find the Gowers and Lambs of this world in a casino than a gym, but if it was a toss-up between going out with them to face the Windies or some bodybuilder with no balls then there is only one way you would want the coin to fall.

Fletcher, D

I didn't know what to expect from Duncan Fletcher when he first tipped up in the England job but I knew he had a reputation as being a bit of a hard man because a couple of the Glamorgan lads had tipped me off. I was to find out just how hard he was only days into our relationship.

Although I am pretty fit naturally, it might be fair to say that I didn't like showing just how fit during England training sessions. If you show the management you are capable of running round the ground five times they will want you to do it ten. So it's best to keep that particular light under a bushel.

In South Africa in 1999 we were playing a warm-up game before the first Test and Fletcher insisted that we do fielding practice after each day's play. To be honest the last thing you want after a hot day in the field is a catching session and Fletcher's sessions were pretty brutal. He would give each player ten catches — not hit straight at them but thrown from side to side so that you had to run.

My work avoidance strategies are usually spot on but this time the coach definitely had my number. I figured that if I threw the ball back wide of him I would get a it more time to get my breath back before the next one arrived. Unfortunately Fletcher had other ideas.

So he put one of the boys to act as a backstop for my wild throws and proceeded to make me sweat. Every catch he gave me was just out of reach and by the time he had run out of balls I was lying in a heap on the floor absolutely knackered.

He didn't say a word. He just picked up his stuff and walked back to the dressing room, leaving his left-arm spinner sobbing on the ground and the rest of the lads pissing themselves on the balcony.

Good judge of a player though. Most of his selectorial hunches have come off and in the cases of Michael Vaughan and Marcus Trescothick spectacularly so, and in contrast to Ray Illingworth his man-management skills are top class.

He has a very good rapport with Nasser Hussain and they have steadied the ship of English cricket a bit. Remember we were officially the world's worst team in 1999 after the loss to

New Zealand so he has made a difference. We are no nearer beating Australia but we are not the only country in the world which has problems against them.

He is big on the team ethic and although I didn't play too much cricket under him for England I was very impressed when he insisted that the boys should all stay together and have a few beers straight after a game instead of going their separate ways. And on tours when the boys have a night out Fletcher goes out and gets pissed with them. Any coach who does that gets my vote straight away.

Fletcher, K

Keith Fletcher bore the brunt of most of my misdemeanours at international level, having to put up with me going AWOL in the Caribbean and into a psychiatric unit in Australia. But he bore up remarkably well and was a bit unlucky to lose his job when Emperor Illingworth decided he wanted to be both coach and chairman of selectors.

Unfortunately we could never quite take his team talks seriously because of his voice and the way words like "prat" became "pwat" when they fell out of his mouth. He also used to get names of players mixed up, rather like Lord Ted Dexter did when he referred to Malcolm Devon, and once introduced Paul Allott as John Arlott.

Selection meetings could be a bit of a lottery if two players with similar names were in the running for a place. According to Athers, he wanted to take someone called Martin McCaddick to Australia once. No wonder Martin McCague, who ended up on the tour, was so mixed up when he got off the plane.

But he lived and breathed English cricket and bowled every ball with you when you were on the pitch so I felt a bit sorry for him on that tour when we lost a couple of games early on. *The Sun* put a picture of him on their back page with a pair of rabbit ears drawn on. They also helpfully printed the fax number of the hotel and told their readers to fax the Gnome and tell him what they thought of him and the team. Naturally they flowed faster than the runs of an Aussie batsman's blade and Fletch could hardly get out of his room for all the fax paper. All a bit harsh.

Flintoff

Freddie Flintoff has already been struck by the curse of being labelled the Next Botham but unlike most of the blokes who have been called Beef Mark Two he seems to have survived relatively unscathed.

He has got through the knocks about his weight, got a Test hundred and looked the most consistent of England's bowlers during the last World Cup. He has even been on the front page of the tabloids for his three-in-a-sauna romps down in Kiwi Country a couple of years back. The boy clearly has a talent for the big stage.

The term allrounder would have described Fred's physique when he first got in the England team but he has cut down on the kebabs and light ales and got himself into shape.

It is just a shame that the English authorities did not look after him as well leading up to the last Ashes tour. Fred came back early from the trip because of hernia trouble but he should have had that sorted out in the summer. Instead, England made him play in the third Test against India and delayed the operation. So England's best allrounder went down under a quarter fit and with no chance of playing in the hardest Test series around. What genius came up with that?

Lord MacLaurin had a pop at Freddie saying that he and Goughie had been on the sauce when they should have been been in the gym but if they had been looked after by the board they would have been on tour instead of being stuck in Lilleshall.

Freemantle Doctor

Perth is no place for a slow bowler. The pitch is reckoned to be one of the quickest in the world so as soon as you arrive at the ground the opening bowlers are charging round like they have taken some macho pills. They always bowl too short and all turn into Jeff Thomson on speed but for spinners the place is basically a glorified graveyard. Even the tubby Australian leggie can hardly buy a wicket there.

There are three strange things about playing in Perth. The

pitch is always referred to as the quickest in the world but for a while this was not strictly true. But it was back to its fastest on the last Ashes tour after being relaid. Apparently a fan had taken some of the turf when it was dug up in the eighties and the groundsman used cuttings from that for his new surface. Alan Titchmarsh, eat your heart out.

It is also one of the hottest places on earth to play cricket and at around lunch-time you feel like you're standing in the Gobi desert. Your throat is dry, you are sweating buckets and your head is ringing. It is no wonder the Aussies like chucking the amber nectar down their throats.

Until the Freemantle Doctor starts to blow. This, according to the brochures, is a "cool afternoon breeze that blows in from the sea." My arse. It is more like a hurricane and as soon as that starts gusting at least one of the quick lads will have had a guts full and will be scurrying off to the dressing room to change his shirt after discovering he is not Thommo reincarnated.

That leaves an end for the token spinner in the side to plug up. Talk about the short straw. It makes you feel like you are the last one to pull at a party, your mates have walked off with the tasty crumpet and all that's left in the fridge is a bottle of sweet sherry.

The Doctor can actually help a spinner because bowling into the wind can help you give the ball a bit more air — but by the time the twirlers get on in Perth the scoreboard reads 300-2 and Godzilla is batting at the other end.

Full Bung

Another way of describing a full toss but could also apply to people checking their brown envelopes have enough folding stuff in them after a dodgy one-dayer.

Is For ...
Gabba
Gatting
Getty
Gooch
Gough
Gower
Grand
Gravy
Gus

Gabba

The first time I went to Australia I thought the GABBA was Australia's champion loudmouth but it is in fact a ground in Brisbane in the suburb of Woolloongabba — better known as the scene of Beefy's slaughter of the Aussie bowling in 1986.

The British Lions lads played there in 2001 but they had two advantages over me when I turned up there to play for the first time in a Test match. They are all about 19 stone and the crowd are about 50 yards away for a rugby match — and they won which helps to keep the home supporters quiet for a while.

When Athers, skippering an Ashes party for the first time, sent me down to field by the GABBA Hill I had a rough idea what was coming my way — this was after all the same crew who once sent a pig onto the pitch with the legend 'Eddie Hemmings', a tribute to the weighty spinner, daubed on his side.

I think Athers knew what he was doing as well. He also knew that the playing surface at Brisbane is slightly larger than the MCG so when I was stationed on the fence I was about 90 metres away from Steve 'Bumper' Rhodes behind the timbers. With the ball in your hand it looks about 900 metres and uphill. I don't know how the Aussie fielders ping it in from there.

The stick I copped was unbelievable — but what can you do. You can't exactly jump into the crowd *a la* Eric Cantona and deck the nearest heckler or offer to take 10,000 screaming Aussies out the back of the stands. So the best bet is collar up, cap down, sunglasses on and hope to get a few wickets without letting the ball between your legs for four. Taking zip for 70-odd in the first dig did not do my confidence a lot of good but four-for in the second almost shut them up.

When Athers sent Goochie down there all he got from the crowd was stuff like "have another tinny and you'll look like Merv." When Gatt, on his last trip, was sent west for a spot of sentry duty he got "who the **** is Father Christmas." And all the time the old boys were getting the treatment I had to avoid catching Athers' eye in case he put me back on the fence.

Gatting

Mike 'Jabba the Hutt' Gatting was a top pub captain. That may sound like stating the obvious but growing up with his Middlesex team meant that you learned most of your cricket in the snug bar at the pub round the corner from Lord's listening to the old pros chatting about the game. That's my kind of a school lesson.

He would explain bowling plans, using old fag packets and pickled eggs and I was like a sponge, for the beer, the chat and the knowledge the experienced pros passed on. If I was to ask a young left armer now if he wanted to have a couple of pints to work out how he is going to bowl at some West Indian he has never seen before I would probably get a funny look.

Most of them are straight off to the gym after a day's play to see how much they can bench press and are immersed in sweat instead of the game.

We didn't spend all of our spare time with Gatt being matey in the boozer because he shares a mean streak with his look-a-like from the film 'The Return Of The Jedi,' If you had been out of line he could dish out the most fearful bollockings. But he never bore a grudge — after giving you a 20 minute tongue lashing he would waddle out of the door and forget all about it.

Gatt's reign as Middlesex captain also coincided with quite a few of my more memorable indiscretions, which involved brushes with everyone from the Middlesex hierarchy to my ex-bird's old man. But every time I'd been a naughty boy he would dish out the bollocking, walk straight out and tell the waiting press or the committee what a great bowler I was and that he was right behind me. He once frogmarched me to the barbers to have my ponytail cut off and looked on me as a sort of naughty nephew.

On one occasion he suspended me from the Middlesex team for a week after I had chucked my toys out of the pram when I got hit for a six and tried to put the blame on Gatt for not having a fielder in the stand.

I was just bowling crap and I knew it. Gatt knew it and banned me for seven days. He stuck to it, too, and although a lot of players would relish a free week in the middle of the season my absence coincided with a club trip to Dublin where Middlesex were playing Ireland in the NatWest. None of the black stuff for Tuffers that time. Cheers Gatt.

When things went pear-shaped for me on my return from the Caribbean in 1994 he stood up for me when the boys in the Long Room were ready to drum me out of the club — and God knows where I would be now if Gatt hadn't backed me.

He could bat a bit too and was one of a group of really big men — Lamb, Gooch, Gower, Botham — I was lucky enough to play with. These boys were not scared of anything and could think on the hoof if things weren't going according to plan.

In 1991, when he was like a man on a mission and almost tried to score all of Middlesex's runs on his own, Dessie Haynes was touring with the Windies, Ramps was with England for most of the summer and only Mike Roseberry and Paul Weekes could score a run. Gatt was hobbling around with a dodgy back and a knackered hamstring and still weighed in with more than 2000 runs. The season was going nowhere and we were down with the dead men for most of the year but he still tucked into the bowling as if it was one of the buffet lunches at Lord's.

Getty

When Sir Paul Getty died in April 2003 cricket lost one of its biggest supporters and the England side lost some of the best days out you could ever have on tour. He was out in the West Indies to watch us on the 1998 tour and invited us all for a day on his boat.

To call it just a boat would be like describing the Mona Lisa as just a painting and I'd not been on anything like it before or since. We could have played the Test match on the deck it was so big, and the pitch would have been a bit flatter. Normally you would give official trips like this a wide berth but this was one not to miss. There was food and drink everywhere and the boat was more like a cruiser than a yacht.

I played a few games at his private ground in Wormsley which he had built to the same spec as The Oval and I always jumped at the chance to get down there. You could turn up and see Shane Warne bowling at Mick Jagger, it was brilliant. He also helped transform Lord's by dipping into his own pockets to help out with building the Mound Stand. Not bad for a bloke who was once Surrey president.

Gooch

My relationship with Goochie on my first Ashes trip made Gatt's ruck with Shakoor Rana look like 'Love Story,' He probably thought I was a disrespectful, jumped-up little oik. In fact, I know he thought that because he told me so, but more than ten years on I would like to think we get on and he knows I could bowl a bit of respectable left-arm spin.

But even when I was pratting around I always had massive respect for Gooch. He is the best and most determined batsman I have played with or against — no question — and to see him getting pumped before going into bat against Marshall and Ambrose was like watching George Foreman warm up for a big fight.

When Michael Vaughan got to the top of the batting world rankings recently it was no surprise to find out that the last Englishman to be on the top of the pile was Goochie a decade before.

He would strap his pads on like a gladiator preparing to go in and face the lions and would be lost in a cocoon of concentration as he talked to himself. It was massively reassuring to know he was going out to face the bullets in front of you.

When you walked out onto the pitch with players like Gooch it didn't matter who you were playing or where. You could be in front of 100,000 in India or on a death trap in Jamaica and you knew you would be in the game and it wouldn't go completely tits up because the ball wasn't swinging or their quicks were a bit tasty.

Although I didn't play in the game, Gooch's ton against the West Indies in 1991, I am told, was about as good a knock as you will ever see. The Windies attack was Ambrose, Walsh, Patterson and Marshall all sprinting in on a Headingley green-top, and without middling the ball, Gooch made 154 not out from 250-odd. The next highest English score was 27.

Throughout his England captaincy he led by example and expected people to follow, but when he looked over his shoulder sometimes he didn't have too much company. So the ultimate pro must have been tearing his soon-to-be transplanted hair out when I bowled into view on that tour to Oz.

He had a finger operation and missed the first Test, and as I wasn't pulling up any trees at that stage of the trip we went into the first Test at Brisbane with four quicks and Allan Lamb standing in as skipper. We were trounced. Goochie came back for the rest of the series but he fell out spectacularly with his rookie spinner when I looked like I had refused to shake his hand after I'd taken my first Test wicket (Matthews ct Hemmings b Tufnell 128). Actually I didn't see him coming in my excitement but the little misunderstanding only added to his problems.

All that running he did, lapping the ground when he was out and sprinting back to the hotel instead of getting on the bus meant that he was fit enough to bat all day. He didn't just get a flashy 120 and scoop one up to mid-off, he would get big, big hundreds and then big, big doubles and trebles.

However, just because he could train or net for 24 hours a day did not mean we all wanted to have cricket shoved down out throats morning, noon and night, and when he was skipper the odd night on the beer might have made the squad a bit happier. I might have given the impression that I was a streetwise cockney wide boy when I went to Australia with Gooch's side but I don't mind admitting that by the end of the trip I didn't know my arse from my elbow.

Naughty boy nets and so-called jankers games do not do anyone any good because your whole mind-set is up the spout.

On the flip side I only played with Gooch when he had been on the Test scene for more than 15 years and he was probably working harder to stay fit than he did when he was slightly younger. Some of the things that Goochie and his best mate Embers got up to in their early days on the county circuit are enough to make your eyes water.

Gough

When we had to choose songs to walk out to in one-day internationals Goughie lived up to one of his other nicknames, Dazzler, by picking 'Walking on the Sunshine' by Katrina and the Waves. That sums him up. He is a super confident, extroverted and positive bloke and that comes through in the way he plays the game.

On the 1994-5 tour to Australia we really thought we had unearthed, whisper it quietly, the Next Botham after he smashed a fifty and took six wickets in Sydney. That day everything he tried came off and he even got Mark Taylor out caught and bowled with a leg break.

From that moment on he was a hero with the Barmy Army and even Goochie said that having Gough in the dressing room was like having the legendary Beef around. Ray Illingworth soon knocked that remark on the head.

Shortly afterwards, he had the first knock back of his career when he got injured playing in a one-dayer and missed the rest of the tour. But he came back and in the late nineties there were, as *Wisden* put it, two England teams — "one with Darren Gough and one without."

Just like Gus Fraser, though, he has struggled to keep himself in one piece and has only played in about half of England's Tests since his debut. If we had had a pace attack of Gough, Caddick and Fraser all fit, firing and most importantly in Gus's case picked, then England might have won a lot more cricket matches in the last six or seven years.

One match we did manage to win, although the circumstances have since been shown to be a bit murky, was at Centurion Park in South Africa on Nasser's first tour as captain. The Boks were 155 for six on the first day and that was how it stayed for three days while it pissed down with rain. Goughie was convinced that there wouldn't be any play on the fifth day and got involved in a drinking match against the Welsh golfer Ian Woosnam who was playing in the Johannesburg Open. I had not been picked for the match and was able to enjoy a few bottles of Castle knowing that I wouldn't have to bowl the next day.

For England's premier strike bowler however waking up still pissed to see the sun blazing down on the ground was definitely not what the doctor ordered. Especially when Hansie Cronje offered Nasser the chance of a total to chase if both sides forfeited an innings.

So game on then. The series was dead in the water but we could nick a win and at least get back a bit of pride. We didn't know at the time that Cronje was involved in all sorts of skullduggery with illegal bookies and couldn't really believe it when he offered to set us 249 to win in 79 overs.

Nasser knew full well that the Dazzler had been on the sauce the night before and made him bowl about ten overs straight off while South Africa got up to the agreed total. In those circumstances you just have to take your medicine and bowl. If you moan then the bollocking from the skipper will make your hangover seem very trivial.

Fair play, then, to Goughy. He got through his stint and then maintained his golden bollocks image by hitting the winning runs. Talk about getting away with it.

Like most great players you only realise how good someone is when they are not there, and England missed Goughy badly in the last Ashes series when they took a punt on his fitness, and even more badly during the World Cup.

He is the best death bowler in England by a distance and the Aussies wouldn't have fancied their chances of beating England in the last stages of the World Cup pool game if the Rhino had been charging in to bowl at the death.

His start to the season after the injury was typical Gough. Six wickets, a win for Yorkshire and England's best bowler back in the headlines. I hope we haven't seen the last of him as a force in international cricket because box office Test players don't grow on trees in this country.

Gower

Gower was the odd-one out of the Three G's. Where Gooch and Gatting could pummel the bowling, Gower would murder you gracefully as if he was conducting an orchestra at the London Palladium. But I always fancied bowling at him because he gave you a chance to get him out and didn't bully you in the way that Viv Richards or Gooch could.

But he and Gooch had about as much in common as Gatt and Rosemary Conley of hip and thigh diet fame. They were both brilliant players in their own ways and Gower was champagne to Goochie's brown ale on and off the field but their Test stats are fairly similar, proving there is more than one way to skin a cat.

I think Gooch was suspicious that some of Gower's bad habits would rub off on me, although I've never made a habit of getting to 120 and getting myself out with a casual flick down the leg side.

However, even Gower would probably admit that hiring a couple of Tiger Moths in the middle of an Ashes tour that was going pear-shaped was probably not the smartest thing he has ever done. He paid about 30 quid to go up in the air and had another grand to shell out when he landed. But he had 13 years of Test cricket behind him whereas his co-pilot John Morris was on his first trip and the whole business probably cost a very good player a shot at a decent Test career.

Gower was so laid back he was virtually horizontal, and when he was summoned by tour manager Peter Lush for his bollocking he stayed and finished dinner and made Gooch, Stewart and the rest of the disciplinary mob wait for the morning until they could haul him over the coals.

His relationship with the captain, however, broke down terminally when he threw his wicket away in the Adelaide Test. Gooch had been sweating his nuts off trying to keep us in the game (eventually making 87 and 117). His face went black with rage when he saw Lubo chip one from Craig McDermott straight down Big Merv Hughes' neck at long-leg the ball before lunch after making a breezy 11. Gooch was at the other end and was fuming when he came in for lunch and his mood was not improved when Allan Lamb defended Gower by piping up, "You know what Lubo's like, you have to take the rough with the smooth." The captain looked roughly like he wanted to punch Gower's lights out.

The grind of the circuit was just not Gower's bag and

his record in internationals is better than his county one. Interestingly Michael Vaughan and Marcus Trescothick are in a similar situation. He just could not seem to get up for the run-of-the-mill games but he is not the only player in history to be like that.

The greatest Gower story of all time came when he was a youngster at Leicestershire and had been hauled over the coals for his dress sense — he was obviously not the dapper chap he is now. So he turned up at breakfast in the full penguin suit leaving captain Ray Illingworth choking on his bacon and eggs as he was asking him if he had just come in from a night out. Wish I had seen that one.

Grand

I haven't got the best memory in the world and am the first to admit that some stages of my career passed in a bit of a blur but I can say with absolute certainty that I had a few beers on 29 July 2001.

The reason I remember the day so well is that I got my 1,000[th] first class wicket when I bowled Durham's Aussie batsman Martin Love at Lord's. After spending the whole of my adult(ish) life, up to then, purveying left-arm twirlers for a living I had finally hit four figures.

I slept on 999 and was a bit fidgety when we got to the ground. I just wanted to get my hands on the ball and get it over and done with. Luckily the pitch was turning a bit and big Gus got me on pretty sharpish. I managed to get my fourth ball through Love's defences and will admit to going a bit potty.

That put me in some pretty decent company. At the time, of those playing the game, only Allan Donald, Phil DeFreitas and Wasim Akram had more (Devon Malcolm has also got his grand now). I'll settle for that trio — not a spinner among them.

To be classed as an allrounder you have got to get more runs than wickets and I am pleased to report that I also crept past the 2,000 run barrier before finishing. Gatt used to get 2,000 in a season — it took me 16 years!

Gravy

God knows what the stewards would have made of Gravy if he had ever pitched up at Lord's, but it would have been long odds against him seeing out the day's play without being hauled down to the local nick.

Gravy used to turn up at the Recreation Ground in Antigua wearing outfits that would have done justice to some of Soho's finest ladies of the night. Although the grey beard looks out of place on top of some of the silky numbers he wears the pins aren't that bad.

On top of the threads, or lack of them, he used to hang off the stands and lead the singing that made Antigua one of the more entertaining places to play. It took your mind off the scoreboard that usually rattles round at a frightening rate of knots when you play there. And as he gyrated around the boundary the reggae from Chickie's disco would pump out like you were in the middle of a carnival. Which is great but you try bowling at Carl Hooper when you're half-stoned from the smoke wafting across the ground and an ageing transvestite is questioning your manhood.

He 'retired' a couple of years ago and marked the occasion by walking round the ground like some old queen wearing a wedding dress and waving a wand. There were posters round the stadium urging him not to go. Curtly Ambrose and Courtney Walsh were on the verge of retiring and were doing a virtual lap of honour round the cricketing world which lasted a couple of years but the big story in the West Indies was Gravy hanging up his tutu. Our fans may be the Barmy Army but this bloke was absolutely barking. Curtly, Viv and Richie were the kings of the island but Gravy was the face of Antigua.

Gus

After 18 years changing next to Gus Fraser in dressing rooms all over the world for Middlesex and England it was a bit of shock to turn round one day and find that the spottiest arse in cricket was not perched on the bench next to me.

I knew a while before that he would not be around for

much longer. I was fielding at mid-off on one of those days you only get in Durham when the big man — coming to the end of another marathon spell and with cheeks getting redder by the second — turned to me and said, "Bugger this Tuffers, I'm getting too old for this."

I thought he and I formed a pretty good partnership, especially for England when we had to bottle a game up, and he was always the first to put his hand up to bowl into the teeth of a howling gale or at Lara when he was 90-odd not out. The Aussies could be 200-0 or 80-8 and Gus would always run in as if it was his last game.

He was taken for granted too much by England and we only realised how valuable he was to the team when he wasn't there. He was appallingly treated by a succession of selectors and one episode in 1999 summed up how much the national team would take the piss out of Good Old Reliable Gus.

Middlesex were playing against Somerset in Taunton when Gus got the call to join the England squad at Lord's as we were preparing to play New Zealand. He drove 130 miles or so before he got a call on the mobile telling him he wasn't needed really and could turn round and go back to the west country. I'm no expert in man-management but that can't be any way to treat one of your best bowlers.

To make matters worse he would have gone to London the day before but his kit was in the pavilion at Taunton — which was locked. It could only happen in England. The fact that they half-expected him to drive all the way to Lord's then put the ball on a sixpence shows he should have been in the side all along. But he just shrugged his shoulders and got on with it.

The way he fought back from very serious injury was as brave as it was predictable and although he was never going to knock anyone's head off he always gave the batsmen something to think about and not a lot to hit. Without the injuries and selectors pissing him about I would have backed him to take 400 Test wickets and be remembered as an all-time great.

Definitely not what you would call a natural athlete though. If you were building a fast bowler from scratch you wouldn't put many parts of Gus's anatomy in the mix. It didn't make

The skipper informs Gus Fraser he's bowling uphill and into the wind again

Shane Warne celebrates like you expect Aussies to celebrate...

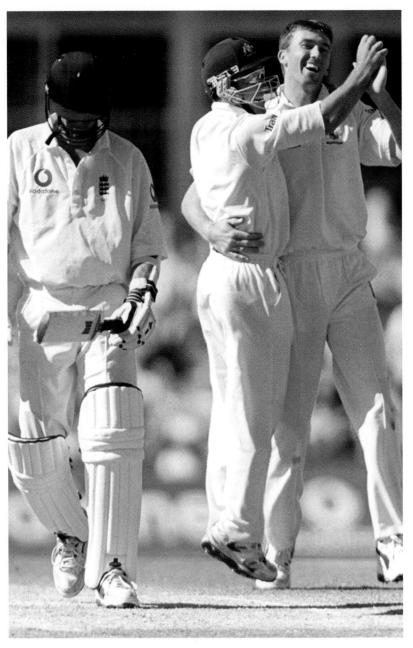

...rather than ballroom dancing like Justin Langer (helmet) and Glenn McGrath. Mind you, McGrath had just got me out

I've got to eat what!!!

ducking bouncers any easier when he was batting as Des Haynes constantly reminded him before one trip to the Caribbean. He duly got peppered but typically didn't moan once.

More than once I thought he would collapse coming up to bowl, and the journalist Martin Johnson memorably described Gus coming in to bowl as looking like someone whose braces had got stuck in the sightscreen. Despite his lumbering approach, the figures in the book stack up and show that he was one the most effective English bowlers of the last 20 years. And they would have been so much better but for the attitude of Mr Raymond Illingworth and Gus's dodgy hip.

I can't work out how Gus had offended the great Yorkshireman but when the Aussies saw the tour party for the 1994-5 trip down under they must have wet themselves laughing.

A look at our bowling attack would hardly have given the likes of Mark Waugh the shakes. The quick bowlers were Joey Benjamin, Phil DeFreitas, Darren Gough, Martin McCague and Devon Malcolm. No disrepect to that lot but with the possible exception of Goughy you would have Fraze in front of the lot of them.

Gus shrewdly went to Australia anyway to play a bit of grade cricket and once the inevitable happened and the quicks started dropping like flies he was drafted in for the third Test in Sydney. I have never been so relieved to see that spotty arse in my life — and he nearly won us the Test match taking five for 73.

David Lloyd knew that England were not a good enough side to leave someone like Gus on the sidelines and he was proved right on the tour to the West Indies in 1998. The same bowler, who Illy didn't think was up to Test cricket, took 32 wickets in the series at just under 20.

One of the many similarities between Gus Fraser and an elephant is that he never forgets. On that Windies tour in 1998 he was doing his usual impression of a robot, pitching six out of six on off stump while the batsmen tried to slog him.

Lara skied Gus to Athers at mid-off and Gus went bananas. Getting the world's best batsman out is usually cause for mild celebration but Fraze completely lost it — punching the air and behaving as if we had won the World Cup. When he was asked what the hell was going in he said, "That gives me one more Test wicket than Illingworth."

Interestingly, he was picked for the trip because we had a lot of green bowlers and Bumble thought Gus could help out coaching them. He banged onto them about stamina, growling that he was not going to bowl their overs at the end of the day. It worked and he would have had a great future in coaching if he hadn't been offered a job writing about the game for one of the broadsheets. A great bowler and a great bloke.

Is For ...
Hand Action
Handled Ball
Hanging Your Bat Out
Harare
Hat-trick
Hawk-eye
Helmet
Hick
Hit The Splice
Hook
Hop Skip And Jump
Howzat?
Hussain

Hand Action

People get the wrong idea when you talk about hand action in cricket circles but the quicks are always harping on about their, er, wrist position. This doesn't mean all seamers are tossers but they do get some funny looks in the pub.

Handled Ball

There are enough ways to get yourself out without this one and it is amazing how a soppy dismissal like this triggers off a collapse.

When Goochie indulged in a bit of handiwork in the 1993 Test at Old Trafford it was the beginning of the end for England. The fact that he had made 133 when he flicked Merv Hughes' delivery away is usually forgotten.

When Steve Waugh, who hates getting out in any fashion, was fingered for handling the ball in Madras in 2001 the Aussies went down like a house of cards, losing seven wickets for zip and the decisive third Test in the process. The moral is keep your hands off your balls lads.

Hanging Your Bat Out

Hanging your bat out to dry is a good way to get into the captain's bad books but something I took at least ten years to master. If your bat is miles away from your body then you've got no chance of getting hit by the fast-approaching missile.

You don't last as long as I did as a pro cricketer without being a master of self-preservation and this is one way to get back in the pavilion without any lasting damage.

Harare

You will never see teams bowl their overs quicker than they do in Harare. Old Robert Mugabe's pile is a few yards down the road from the Harare Sports Club. It might look a quaint old place but there is nothing quaint about the secret police or the curfew. Bowling 12 overs an hour out there is not good for your health so the spinners are always on in the last session so everyone can get back to their hotel before the witching hour. And the hotel is the best place to be; Harare is no place for a night out. I'll never forget the last time I was there. The board had ruled that no other halves would be allowed on tour because apparently the tour party to South Africa the year before had had more babies in it than a maternity unit. Good old sensitive Ray Illingworth had decreed the travelling circus was too much of a distraction so Athers decided on the no-spouse policy.

A couple of the lads were a bit miffed but you're out playing for England and doing your job so that's that as far as I'm concerned. But it was really taking the piss when we spent Christmas day in the Holiday Inn. Nothing against the place which is an OK hotel but it's not the top-notch Sheraton. Guess where the ECB bigwigs stayed?

It was also the scene of one of the biggest humiliations in English cricket. After drawing the Test series in 1996, we wrapped up a 3-0 reverse in the one-dayers by losing two on the spin in Harare. Eddo Brandes, a chicken farmer, got a hat-trick and the press had a field day. "Cluck up" was one of the less imaginative headlines but a huge cluck up it was.

Hat-trick

I never got a hat-trick in any form of cricket — I can't even get my kids out three times in a row nowadays — but I did have the pleasure of denying Mr Shane Warne the chance to get four from four in a Test. And Craig McDermott owes me a large drink for giving up my wicket like I did.

In Melbourne in 1994 Warnie was irresistible. He had already taken 11 wickets in the first Test in Brisbane and had picked up another half a dozen at the MCG in our first dig.

In the second innings he completed his first hat-trick. Daffy DeFreitas was LBW, Goughie caught behind and the bowler's eyes lit up when he saw the next batsman coming in. Big Devon Malcolm had somehow got the nod over me, went in at number ten and it looked like happy days for Warnie.

Sure enough Devon scooped one up, which was brilliantly caught by David Boon at short leg and with me at number 11 Warnie was odds-on for four in four balls. Except he can't count to six and when the umpire called over he knew that I wasn't going to be around for long and his chance to make even more history was gone. I duly nicked one to the keeper, hanging my bat out in time-honoured fashion, and Warnie had to settle for a mere hat-trick. Mind you if you took four from four and the last two were Malcolm and Tufnell I don't think you would be bragging about it for too long.

Hawk-eye

Hawk-Eye was developed by some boffins who were more used to dealing with missiles and it certainly delivered a bombshell when it arrived on Channel Four's coverage of the Test matches.

It proved one thing beyond doubt. That the best umpires in the world basically get the tight LBW decisions right. It's wrong when they show that Hawk-Eye thinks the ball is going on to hit the stumps and the ump has given the batsman not out.

That just makes the officials look stupid and they might be right anyway. Years of experience in the game and of certain pitches gives them a decent shout at getting it right even if the scientists say otherwise.

Helmet

An absolutely vital part of equipment. I remember seeing Viv Richards coming out and not wearing a helmet and thinking he was a raving madman but he could bat like no one else and thought of it as an insult to his manhood if he had to wear one. If a batsman walks out without one now it looks like a red rag to a bull for most fast bowlers. Jonty Rhodes was certainly glad he had one on when he was cleaned up by Devon Malcolm.

I think Richie Richardson was the last Test player to bat in a cap against the quicks instead of donning a lid. If you don't wear one now you are either a genius or an absolute nutter.

Hick

On his day, and I should know because I was at the other end often enough, Graeme Hick was the most destructive player of his generation and although he didn't always do the business in Tests he was not someone I ever looked forward to bowling at.

Although the English authorities changed their qualification rules to stop New Zealand getting him he still did not play for England early enough. If they could have chucked him in before they did, say in 1988, when he was battering county attacks around for fun, it might have been a different story and he could have been right up there with the Laras and Tendulkars of this world.

Speaking as a bloke who regarded batting as a bad way of interrupting your kip in the dressing room I can only look at his stats in awe. More than 100 hundreds, 1,000 runs before the end of May, hitting 405 which could have been about 800 if his skipper had not declared and getting to 50 tons at a younger age than Bradman himself.

They said he couldn't play pace but he played it pretty well when he hit 172 off the Windies attack at New Road to bring up his personal 1,000 in 1988. I wish that I had been that bad playing against the quick stuff.

So when he finally got into the England side against the West Indies back in 1991 the whole country expected him to go out and treat Curtly Ambrose and the rest of their bowlers in the same way he treated the trundlers on the county circuit. And when he didn't he was dropped, then brought back, dropped and brought back for the next ten years. He was discarded then recalled almost as many times as me and Ramps. At the last count I think we were neck and neck with each other after being dropped about ten times each. That doesn't do much for your self-confidence I can tell you.

He had such a huge presence when you bowled to him at New Road in the championship that it was surprising when his shoulders sagged a bit as soon as he got into a Test. At least he could laugh at himself though. Once when he was having a bad trot he was caught cleanly at slip but the umpire didn't give it out. After that he could not lay a bat on the ball and when he was eventually dismissed he came back into the dressing room and said, "I would have walked for that catch if I'd have known I was going to make such a prick of myself."

If Athers had not declared at Sydney with Hicky on 98 not out it might have been the innings that finally convinced him he could do it against the top boys. But now we will never know.

Hit the Splice

If a bowler is said to hit the splice hard it really means he is not very quick but gets a bit of bounce occasionally. The so-called heavy ball that thumps into the top of the bat, near the batsman's gloves, was one of Gus Fraser's specialities. After his serious hip injury we knew he was back when the heavy ball returned to his armoury.

Hook

As you probably know already the hook shot was not in my armoury. To be honest I was more interested in getting out of the way of the ball than getting in line like someone in front of a firing squad.

My admiration of Ian Botham only grew when I saw him hooking people with his eyes shut. And it grew even more when I realised the bowler was Dennis Lillee.

Hop Skip and Jump

People used to take the mickey out of my run-up but the old 'hop, skip and jump' routine as I ran into bowl was a vital part of my game. Most bowlers have little routines to make sure they arrive at the crease in the same way for each delivery. Some swap the ball from one hand to the other while Warnie tosses himself a few catches as he sets himself.

If my hop, skip and jump all landed in the right place then it was odds on that I would be in the right place when I had to bowl. If they didn't then I would more than likely bowl a no ball.

It might have looked like I was dying for a piss but it helped settle me as I got to the wicket.

Howzat?

This is a usually fruitless question to the man in the white coat although you don't hear people say 'Howzat' that often nowadays. Most of the blokes just scream 'Howisheeeeeeeeeeeee' before giving the batsman the send off.

Hussain

In 1990 if you asked someone for the definition of Nasser Hussain it would have been — talented, temperamental batsman liable to chuck toys out of pram. (In fact it was rumoured on the circuit that he went berserk so often that the Chelmsford outfield looked like a creche after a kids' birthday party). Definition of Hussain nine years later — England captain and part of the furniture.

I enjoyed playing for Nasser because at the start of our careers we were both seen as troublemaking toe-rags and when I pratted around Nasser knew how to handle me better than some skippers because he had been there, done it and bought the prat t-shirt. He knows what you are going through as a player and he can work with you — although I didn't think much of it when he gave the bowler advice every ball. If you have got to play in a Test match you don't need reminding where to bowl even if you can't get the ball to go there.

Nasser's temperament probably has something to do with the fact that he is really a spinner at heart and we are prone to the odd tantrum. As a kid he was one of the best young leg-spinners in the country and the fact that he has got a bit of a temper is because he is one of us.

He could not even control his tendency to throw a wobbly in his first tour match for England when he refused to walk in the first innings and gave the umpire a stare that Curtly Ambrose would have been proud of when he was fingered in the second dig.

Not a great start if you want to end up as England captain but he got there eventually when Alec Stewart lost the Test captaincy because the one-day side screwed up in the 1999 World Cup (work that one out).

And the first thing he did as England captain was recall the two difficult characters who had been frozen out when Alec was gaffer i.e. Andy Caddick — who successive skippers had found hard to work out — and PCR Tufnell, or as the papers like to call me "the maverick spinner." The other half of the Tantrum Twins, Mark Ramprakash, was there as well (Nasser is a founding member).

Naturally, as I have known Nasser since he was attempting to bowl wrist spin for Forest School against Highgate, I thought, as a senior-ish player I would get a bit of rope. So, in South Africa on his first tour as captain, I took a few liberties with regard to late nights and training. Previous captains would look at my antics and shrug their shoulders saying "Well that's Tuffers for you." Nasser went bananas.

He pulled me to one side and gave me the most fearful bollocking I've had since I was caught smoking behind the bike sheds at primary school.

On and on he went, how he'd put his head on the block to get me on tour, how I was taking the piss and how he'd put me on the first plane back home if I stepped out of line again. Alex Ferguson is famous for the hairdryer treatment he dishes out to players if they arse about but this was Hurricane Naz, in stereo, from four inches.

I knew that he meant it so got my head down for the rest of my stay and Nasser has carried on as single-mindedly as that ever since. Perhaps all those wobblies he threw as a youngster at Essex were in frustration when things weren't perfect and he was not the brat that everyone thought he was.

He was a strong skipper to start with. All captains come in strong and try to impose themselves on the team when they get the job but Nasser came in stronger than most, saying that England had to get tough or we would be lagging behind the Aussies for the next few hundred years. But eventually he got worn down like the rest by having too much responsibility and not having the armoury that he needed to compete with the very best.

When the England players needed a lead over whether to play in Zimbabwe or not they didn't turn to the board because they knew they'd get five-eighths of naff-all out of that shower. So it was Nasser who had to make the running and most of the time during a very tricky period he made the right calls.

The board were obviously happy to let Nasser hang out to dry when the shit was about to hit the fan and they should have got the bullet as well when England were knocked out of the World Cup.

He has broken a few bad runs and England are clearly heading in the right direction thanks to him — it's just that we are not going in that direction as fast as the Australians. England won in Pakistan for the first time since Lord Ted Dexter was captain, and they came from behind to win in Sri Lanka. His side beat the Windies at home for the first time for about 30 years but we still can't win the Ashes.

God knows, though, what was going through his head in Brisbane when he sent the Aussies in and they nearly broke the scoreboard. But when you make a decision like that you have got to pray that your bowlers deliver — ask Sourav Ganguly after he let Australia bat first in the World Cup final. But overall he will go down as a very good skipper who didn't quite have the players around him to do the job against the best side in the world.

It was the right thing for him to pack in the one-day job because as he admitted he was no longer worth his place in the side, and if you're not in on merit you lose the respect of the troops. It should give him a few more years in the Test team and another crack at the Aussies.

Is For ...
ICC
Idiot
Illingworth
Image
Injuries
In My Day
Innings
Inzamam
Irani

ICC

After all my brushes with authority you would think the name of Phil Tufnell would be on the bottom of the list of potential players at a shindig organised by the rulers of cricket.

Imagine my surprise then three years ago when a brown envelope dropped on the doormat at Tufnell Towers with an invitation for me to play in a day-nighter in Dhaka as part of an ICC promotional week. Me, Philip Tufnell, scourge of the cricketing hierachy, an ambassador for the sport? A mere six years after being fined by the ICC for throwing the ball in an aggressive manner? With my colourful past?

More ironically it was a one-day game, between an Asian XI and the Rest of the World, and I hadn't got a look in with the England side for more than three years. Time to buff up the boots and get out to Bangladesh I thought.

For a so-called non-competitive match I couldn't believe that more than 50,000 people turned up to watch but when I saw the batting line-up I had to bowl at I realised why they had come in their droves.

To be frank when I had a peek at the names I wanted to get back on the plane and back into pre-season training. It was definitely not a freebie jaunt with Jayasuriya, Tendulkar, Ganguly, De Silva and Akram oiling their bats in the opposition dressing room.

Sachin Tendulkar and Sourav Ganguly are hard enough to get out once without giving them a life and guess what the representative of the fine art of English slow bowling did? I only managed to drop Tendulkar and Ganguly off my own bowling before finally getting them to hole out in the deep.

Our side was chasing well over 300 and we nearly got there thanks to Michael Bevan playing one of the best one-day innings I have ever seen in my life. Bev knocked up 185 not out off of 132 balls and treated some of the top bowlers in the world as if they were Mickey Mouse merchants.

We finished up a run short but should have won the game because one of Bevan's sixes was given as a four. The TV showed it had carried over the rope and the ICC game ended in a bit of a cock-up. No change there then.

Idiot

My introduction to the searing wit of the Australian crowds came with this corker. Fielding on the boundary as usual, my concentration was broken by one of the spectators shouting out "Tufnell, lend us your brain, we're building an idiot." What a way with words they have down there.

Illingworth

Uncle Raymond and I did not always see eye-to-eye but then I wasn't the only one who found him hard to work out. They reckoned that Mike Brearley had a degree in people and even he would have struggled to fathom Illy. Athers was definitely very suspicious of him when he started and as things turned out Ath was not a bad judge.

When we came back from the West Indies in 1994, the shadow of Illy loomed over our immediate futures like a black cloud over the pitch at the Scarborough Festival.

We had lost the series but had managed to beat the Windies in Barbados, which in those days was not to be sniffed at, but the new supremo of English cricket was not a happy bunny.

The great Yorkshireman had let a few things get into the papers about what he was going to do to the team and frankly a few of the boys were crapping themselves about the arrival on the English scene of this cricketing messiah.

They had brown trousers with good reason as well. When Athers sat down with the selectors to pick a team for the Caribbean he said he wanted to go with some good young players and stick with them for a couple of years. Fat chance in the Whacky World of Raymond.

We went through the mire in the Windies and although I had a pretty good idea that I wouldn't be involved in the upcoming Tests, least of all because I'd fallen out with Middlesex temporarily, a player like Graham Thorpe should have been a stone-bonking certainty for the summer.

Illy, as usual, knew better of course. He hadn't met half of the side and all of a sudden he was a bloody expert on the lot of us. Of the batsmen who had been dodging the bullets in the

Caribbean all winter only Judge, Stewie, Athers and Hicky got a game in the first Test against New Zealand. Matthew Maynard, Ramps, Thorpey and Nasser were all given the old Dear John and told to get some runs for their counties. Everyone was pigeon-holed as mad, inconsistent, not tough enough or on the piss. So much for Athers' hopes for the future of English cricket.

Into the void stepped Mr GA Gooch. I have already said that Goochie was the best batsman I've ever had the misfortune to bowl at, but he was not what England wanted then. Aged nearly 41, he duly chalked up 210 against the might of Dion Nash, Gavin Larson and Heath Davis (slightly different from Ambrose and Walsh) and proved absolutely nothing in the process.

Incredibly Thorpey did not get another Test until we played South Africa later in the summer. To no-one's great surprise he made a stack of runs as soon as he was called back into the team. Illy probably claimed the credit for that one as well.

Fortunately, I didn't have too much to do with Illingworth because his reign coincided with one of the less productive spells of my Test career and my form meant that most of the time he was entitled to leave me out of the side. Court appearances and front page headlines for scrapping with my girlfriend's old man didn't endear me to someone like Illy.

He was a Yorkie straight from the old school. So what was he to do with a smoking, cockney twirler from down south who had a bad reputation before he arrived on the scene? Drop him mostly was the answer.

Still you can't expect to be the apple of the boss's eye all the time if you are a spinner but at least I was not the only one to be on the wrong end of his unique management skills.

He idea of geeing up Graeme Hick was to call him soft while his row with Devon Malcolm seemed to rumble on forever with flak flying from both ends. It even got a mention in the Houses of Parliament. I don't know what was said out in South Africa by Illy that time because I was chilling out in north London so we'll call it a draw.

But I do know that Illingworth was wrong not to pick Gus Fraser more often.

It would be fair to say that the pair do not swap Christmas cards these days and Gus would have had plenty more caps and wickets in his locker if Illingworth had rated him as highly as Athers did. Illingworth even went as far as to say that Athers' friendship with Gus had clouded his judgement of the big man as a bowler. I know that Raymond was England captain when they won a series in Australia but that was about 100 years ago in cricketing terms and I'm afraid that picking Martin McCague instead of Big Gus does not mark you down as a shrewdie.

The ball might have flown round people's noses in Australia when John Snow was bowling but by the time we got down there the wickets were much slower and therefore much more suited to someone like Gus. Illy wouldn't listen to anyone who had actually played there more recently and preferred to live in the past and go with his own judgements made 20 years before. Great.

I also couldn't believe it when he didn't come out for the start of his first Ashes trip as our boss and started slagging us off from his house after watching the games on the box.

When you are on a trip like that you need to have everyone backing you – not shouting their mouths off to the press when they are not even within 8,000 miles of the tour. He even watched some of the games from his villa in Spain. To say the boys were not impressed would be a bit of an understatement.

When he did arrive in Australia it was straight out with the 'In my day we could out all six balls on a sixpence' record. That didn't go down well.

He was never high up on Athers' Christmas card list either. On the same trip we heard that Illy had been at a lunch in London where he claimed he had saved the skipper's job after the dirt in pocket affair and that Athers had never even said thank-you. Typically Athers refused to get involved, just bit his lip and got on with it.

Apart from not picking Gus for so long, Illingworth also just about ended the Test career of Robin Smith – at least five years too early. He could have had 100 caps instead of the 62 he ended up with, but apparently he wound up our glorious leader in South Africa with his preference for the high life. England must be a great side to leave out a player like the Judge.

To piss off Thorpe, Smith, Hick, Fraser, Malcolm and Athers, to name just a few, in such a short space of time takes some doing but Raymond managed it. And English cricket suffered for it.

When he started the job I was miles from getting into the team so I wasn't around when he banned mobile phones and sunglasses and got rid of the team chaplain Andrew Wingfield-Digby. The sacking of the chaplain was typical Illingworth.

He played the hard, bloody Yorkshireman trick too often and it made us sick. When you are away on tour and you have a problem who can you talk to? You can't talk to the skipper in case he thinks you've gone bananas and he drops you, and you can't talk to the management for the same reason. So it was quite good to have someone on board who you could have a natter with for ten minutes knowing that it wasn't going to go straight to the men-in-charge. But no. The "We didn't have them in my day so you won't have them now" bollocks resurfaced and that was that.

Still I pissed myself when I saw Alec Stewart on the box standing on the balcony at Trent Bridge wearing a dog collar, a lovely pair of shades and chatting into his mobile. I don't know what Illingworth made of it all but it was one of the few laughs Stewie ever managed to raise.

Image

It is highly unlikely that anyone would ask but if a youngster starting out on a career in cricket wanted any advice from me I would tell them to sort out their image and not get saddled with a bad reputation early on.

If you asked any cricket fan, or non-fan for that matter, about me they would say, "Oh, Tuffers, likes a drink, smokes, couldn't bat or field." I could stay indoors for the rest of my life and still wouldn't get rid of my reputation.

There are plenty of places to go for a drink when you are at a loose end, where your face won't end up in the papers. Once your face does get on the front page it is very hard to shift it and that image as a hellraiser out of the public's and, more importantly, selectors' minds. I had a reputation as a bad tourist — but I played nearly three times as many Tests abroad as I did in England, so I couldn't have been that bad away from home. A couple of incidents on my first Ashes tour meant that I had to carry the label round with me for the rest of my career. Not that I was an angel on any of my England trips, but the bad reputation I created early on hung around me like a bad smell.

Mike Gatting had a reputation as a big eater which is constantly referred to and that implied he was not fit enough to play. I've seen him on a squash court and he didn't look that unfit to me, but the tag stuck.

It even got to the point when the chairman of the ECB would tell me to behave myself as I got onto a plane to fly the flag for England in a Test series. And I was over 30 at the time.

Once you are out of the game you can do what you like, so it is best to keep your nose clean when you are playing. I found that out the hard way.

Injuries

Apart from a bad case of appendicitis, I managed to stay pretty injury free for most of my career, which given my talent for attracting the short stuff is nothing short of a miracle.

Spin bowlers are pretty low maintenance really, but the seamers are not so lucky. Gus was always injured, even when he was playing, but would just bowl through the pain and moan about it to anyone who would listen. Goughie's had more than his fair share of knocks too.

In my last season as a pro I turned my ankle and thought it was the end of the world. I tried my best to get some sympathy out of the boys but they reckoned it was the only thing I turned all year.

In My Day

"In my day" is a phrase guaranteed to send the world's worst insomniac into the Land of Nod, especially when it is uttered with a Yorkshire accent.

When you have spent as much time as I have seeing your bowling disappearing then the last thing you need to hear is how much better English cricket was forty or more years ago. I am sorry boys. It is just not relevant.

Cricket is a very different game now. The rules are even different and players, well most of them, are ten times fitter than they were. You don't see many beer bellies on a Test match pitch anymore and even the spinners have to do the dreaded bleep tests to show how fit they are.

Now that I have stopped playing the game at that level I am hoping to get the chance to do a spot more media punditry after thoroughly enjoying my stint of radio work at the World Cup in South Africa.

But if anyone hears me utter the phrase "in my day" they have my permission to drop me in a jungle full of creepy crawlies, with nothing to eat except raw worms and make me gather logs for a fortnight. Again.

Innings

I very rarely hung around long enough to build an innings and Lord's saw me in full flow with the bat just once. Every dog has its day and all that, so for 107 glorious minutes in 1996 I knew how Viv Richards felt when he was scoring his tons at HQ.

Against the mighty Worcestershire, John Carr and I managed to post a very rare last wicket stand of over 100 of which PCR Tufnell managed 67 not out and top scored for the only time in my life.

The man in the Telegraph said it was the "season's unlikeliest innings" which I thought was a bit harsh but he added that "the days when Tufnell used to clench buttocks against anyone over Graham Thorpe's pace have gone." I will hold my hands up and say that the knock was pre-Glenn McGrath's day at Worcester and post-Neal Radford, while their express bowler that morning was Stuart Lampitt. Lamps used to be fairly sharp although I'll admit that he wasn't Malcolm Marshall and it was a pleasure to ping him to the boundary once or twice.

I am ashamed to admit that the innings did not mark the start of a second career as a batsman and the arse clenching returned in spades in my next game — at Portsmouth against Hampshire when I was rolled over by Botham Mark Two, Son Liam.

At Test level, my best day with the willow came when I managed to hang around with Hicky in Bombay as he was blasting away at the other end.

We managed to put on 68 for the last wicket of which my contribution was a massive two. I hung around for 81 minutes, defying the Indian bowlers with a succession of pushes and prods while Hicky was launching them all over the park but it was my name that ended up in the records section of *Wisden* — for slow batting.

Inzamam

Inzamam used to be a cricketer who was — to put it kindly — built for comfort and his favourite spot during training sessions was behind the sight-screen sitting in a deckchair. So I was a bit shocked to turn up in South Africa for the 2003 World Cup on media duty and see that his green and yellow Pakistani shirt had shrunk by about ten sizes and no longer looked like an oversized Bedouin tent.

A few years back he was christened 'Aloo' by an abusive fan in Canada and, like any student of curry house menus, I was surprised to find someone with the nickname 'Potato' who could hit the ball back past the bowler at the speed of light.

The incident in Canada tickled me. Inzy was on a newly-formed players' disciplinary committee but had to stand down from it after wading into the stands to have a go at the heckler so it could hear the charge against him.

Proving that disciplinary matters would be better handled by players the world over, he was fined a very small percentage of his match fee and told not to do it again. Imagine the outcry if I had walked into the Mound Stand at Lord's and started waving my long-handle around. I would be lucky to stay out of prison.

I first came across Inzy in the 1992 World Cup in Australia and his hitting in the semi-final against New Zealand was awesome — he got 60 from 37 balls and totally took the game away from the Kiwis.

Running between the wickets has never been his strong point but when you can hit the ball like a cross between Tiger Woods and Viv Richards who needs to waste time and energy sprinting up and down the pitch?

I was even more shocked when the new slimline Inzy couldn't buy a run in the first few matches of the World Cup. Cricket is a game for all shapes and sizes, but I think his balance may have been affected by the weight loss. He even squared up to a team-mate when they were playing football the day before their crunch game against Zimbabwe and he's normally as laid back as David Gower. In six group games he did not get into double figures once, which is outrageous for one of the most talented bats around. He should get back on the curries and get back in shape. I mean it never did Gatt's average any harm.

Irani

Ronnie is a top bloke and one of the most positive people you'll meet in the game. If you're 400 behind on first dig and eight down for zip Ronnie will still see a way to win the game — and he has performed some miracles for Essex.

Great county player and can do a job for England in the one-day side. But an international number three batsman? Please. England pursued that ploy for far too long in the winter and it was no help to Ronnie.

In New Zealand in 1996-7, Ronnie had just broken into the team as the bowling allrounder but was having some back trouble which apparently the England medical team did not know about. Things had not been going well for Bumble after his infamous "We flippin murdered 'em" quote in Zimbabwe and the last thing he needed was for one of the lynch pins of the side to go and cripple himself.

Enter Beefy who had an informal agreement with Bumble to help out the quick bowlers without giving up his job commentating with Sky. The Beef, who was Ronnie's hero, quickly went to work on his action before the fax machine spewed out a message from the physio at Essex.

It said that Botham had no business to be fiddling with the

bowling action of an Essex player. Predictably the Beefmeister went absolutely loopy but the whole thing couldn't have done Ronnie any good.

He worked his way back into the one-day team and I was chuffed to see that he has been granted the Freedom of the City of London. I wonder how many of the benefits he will be able to use. He said he will drive a herd of sheep over London Bridge if England's results improve and he is allowed to be hung by a silk cord if he is convicted of a capital offence.

Right down the bottom of the list of privileges he is entitled to is that he can be drunk and disorderly in the City of London and won't get arrested. Now, that could come in handy for one of our nights out.

Is For...
Jaffa
Jag
Jagger
Jockrot
Johannesburg
Johnson
Joke
Joke Bowler
Jonty
Judge
Jug
Jumbo
Jungle

Jaffa

There are a few bowlers around who reckon they could get me out with an orange but a real jaffa is an absolutely unplayable delivery. Most of the genuinely unplayable balls sail past the outside edge because they are, er, unplayable. But you would have to put Warnie's ball to Gatt down as a jaffa and some of Waqar's inswinging yorkers fall into the same category.

Jag

Seamers don't just move the ball back or away nowadays. Any ball that deviates even slightly is said to 'jag' off the seam as if it's doing something different from a couple of years ago.

Jagger

The news that Mick Jagger was a cricket fan made my choice of career a lot easier than it might have been. The enemy of the establishment, regarded as the Anti-Christ by the twin-set and pearls brigade, munching on a cucumber sandwich at Guildford as he watched a Sunday League match — I couldn't believe it. It certainly gave the game a lot more credibility in my eyes when I was mulling over whether to give it another go in my late teens.

But the bloke is a genuine cricket lover and apparently got the late Paul Getty into the game so every cricket fan can be grateful for that. Once when Mick Jagger found out that a tournament from Sharjah was not being broadcast he bought the rights himself so that cricket fans could listen to the games on the internet.

The man who sang 'Sympathy for the Devil' the saviour of England cricket fans? I liked that.

Jockrot

Apart from bouncers and bits of rotten fruit that are lobbed at you by the crowd, jockrot is one of the biggest hazards to face a touring cricketer. Months and months away with haphazard laundry arrangements means that when you come back from an England trip your nether regions have the complexion of corned beef and the missus is accusing you of all sorts.

It takes ages to clear up and her indoors won't let you near her until you have been immersed up to the waist in a barrel of sheep dip. Not a laughing matter.

Johannesburg

I was not picked for the Athers tour of South Africa, (manager R Illingworth) so I missed the skipper batting for nearly 11 hours to save the Wanderers' Test match in 1995. How anyone can bat for that long in their career let alone in one knock is beyond me.

I managed to make it for the next tour when Duncan Fletcher was in charge but I wasn't picked in Jo'burg and any thoughts I had about frittering away my spare time in some seedy bar downtown were soon shot down in flames by our bodyguard.

He was about six-foot tall and six foot wide and as they used to say was obviously a bit tasty with his fists and the big gun he had in his holster. Unbelievably he got mugged outside the hotel after he left his shooter in his room. I didn't venture out after that. The upshot of his advice was to stay indoors unless I wanted to become another crime statistic.

The hotel we stayed in was something else. It was linked to the biggest shopping centre in the southern hemisphere which meant you could get everything you wanted; beers and every sort of food under the sun could be had without even going onto the street. What a nightmare — play for England, travel the world and see interesting places. It was like being stuck in Brent Cross.

The Wanderers ground is mad as well. To get out onto the pitch you have to walk through the crowd protected by chicken wire. You don't normally get a lot of physical abuse at cricket matches but you can see the players are glad the fence is there by the time the South African fans have got warmed up with a few beers in the afternoon.

Merv Hughes completely lost it there once and ended up battering the cage with his bat, so it's probably a good thing that I never played there with my notoriously short fuse or I would have ended up in front of the match referee again.

Johnson

When Richard Johnson took all ten wickets for Middlesex at Derby in 1994, the first time it had been done in England for about 40 years, it should have signalled the start of a long England career. But a back injury and the usual inconsistency by selectors saw to it that it wasn't.

There was nothing false about the ten-for until Gatt stuck Des Haynes on to bowl in a non-wicket taking capacity when Derbyshire were nine down.

Johnno's new-found fame did not last long. A few days later we were playing Northants in the NatWest at Uxbridge and when it was his turn to bat he sprinted down the stairs to receive the applause from the home fans for his history making figures.

The PA announcer said, "The new batsman is John Emburey." Proving you have to make the most of your fifteen minutes of fame because you get forgotten quickly enough.

Still, Johnno got his chance at last against Zimbabwe at Durham and made sure the announcer remembered who he was this time by taking a six for on his Test debut.

Joke

I like having a laugh as much as anyone but I thought the selectors were joking when they picked me for what turned out to be my last Test match at The Oval.

All summer I'd been on the fringes of the squad and the boys in charge decided to sling me in on the flattest pitch of the whole season. They were obviously banking on my ability to turn it on in south London but I wasn't laughing once the Aussies started climbing into my bowling.

Funnily enough I bowled all right and managed to nick the wicket of Matthew Hayden but the strength in depth of the Australian order was brought home to me big time that day.

Caddy managed to ping Justin Langer on the helmet, after he had made a century, and Steve Waugh came in. He got a ton on one leg and his brother Mark got to three figures, so at one stage they had two batsmen on the pitch with tons and one waiting to come in who had already got a century. All you can do is laugh and give thanks that it is the last Test of the series and the bastards will be on their way home soon.

Joke Bowler

Captains put on the joke bowling when they are trying to buy a wicket and the sight of your opening batsman lumbering in with his hat on the wrong way round is usually enough to have the opposition back in the pavilion.

Graham Gooch was a master of this. He could impersonate every bowler around and would come in like Bob Willis with his arms pumping hoping to lure the batsman into a lapse. Geoff Boycott would serve up a few medium pace wobblers which is all right when a game is petering out into a draw but you wouldn't want to pay money to watch it.

Jonty

Jonty Rhodes reinvented the role of the fieldsman and he is a wicket-taker when he is stationed at behind square on the off side.

Some of the lads could not square his high profile religious beliefs with the fact that he sledges like a good 'un and appeals when he knows the batsman is not out. When he was challenged by one of the England lads once he apparently claimed that we are all sinners. That's that one sorted out then.

I always got on all right with him and he clearly learned how to field by attending the Phil Tufnell Fielding Academy. It always gives me a glow of pride to see one of my graduates doing so well for himself.

Rhodes is just the sort of dynamic player who will encourage the kids to play the game so it was good to see him throw in his lot with Gloucestershire's already formidable one-day outfit. He was probably the biggest name in the world that was available for a whole season, so full marks to Glaws for getting hold of him rather than some Aussie third teamer. Anyone who can put bums on seats is worth having around in county cricket these days.

Judge

Robin Smith, or Judge as he is known because his barnet is similar to the wigs used by the top boys in court, is a legend in the game and one of my best mates in cricket. On the pitch he is like a lion and is probably the bravest player I have ever seen when the quicks are firing it in. He used to sit in the dressing room bashing himself on the chest and screaming 'Be strong' to himself before he went out to bat and would rather the ball hit him on the body than go on to his stumps. I actually think he used to enjoy facing the fast bowlers, as if it was some sort of test of his manhood.

He managed to play 45 Tests on the bounce without getting dropped, which is more than I managed in my whole career, and is the sort of sequence that Mark Ramprakash and Graeme Hick dream about.

Then the curse of the spinners got to him. He was left out for The Oval Test in 1993 against Australia (just as I was surprise, surprise, called into the squad for the last match of the summer, although I didn't play) having had a less than successful time against Shane Warne and Tim May. He was hardly alone in that. From that day on Judge was saddled with the notion that he couldn't play spin and once you have got that tag you can never shift it.

Despite his macho, all guns blazing, style on the pitch, off it he is one of the most likeable blokes around and will do anything to help his mates out.

As well as working bloody hard, he likes to play hard but however late he was out he was always able to get into the nets on time the next day. Most of the time I couldn't believe that he was in the nets dodging missiles while I was in the dressing room curled up in a heap nursing my headache.

Once, however, his alarm call let him down after a heavy session on the old rum-and-cokes in the Caribbean and he was late for a practice match against the Leeward Islands.

Athers sent one of the officials, Doug Insole, to the Judge's room to try and get him out of his pit and when he got there Smith was clearly still suffering the effects of the night before. He didn't have a clue where he was or where he should have been and was obviously still half-pissed. He must have been because he calmly invited Insole in for a cup of tea! Not the best career move ever made.

He was good mates with Athers but that did not stop the captain from dropping a bombshell in Judge's own house. Ath was kipping at Judge's place when Lancashire were down playing Hampshire and casually told him over breakfast one day that he was not going to be in the England side for the next Test match. I always knew Atherton had balls of iron but that beat anything he did on the pitch for bravery.

Jug

Another tradition that's gone out of the window in these health conscious days is the one that said a bowler had to buy a jug of the amber nectar at the bar if he took five wickets. There is so little drinking and socialising in cricket after the game now that the last time I took a five-for I had to drink the lot myself.

Jumbo

Coco Jumbo is one of those characters you would only find in the West Indies. He sells bags of peanuts at the Queen's Park Oval in Trinidad – in between giving advice to the touring team and cheering on the West Indies.

He has an army of kids working for him and when he spots a punter in the stands who wants some nuts he pings them over to them like Ricky Ponting attempting a run out. A kid will then appear at the buyer's shoulder to collect the dosh.

I've been there a couple of times and it doesn't matter how far away from his customer he is he always hits the target. If he worked at Lord's he'd be offered a central contract.

Jungle

As an England cricketer you go through plenty of lows but I have never hit the depths of despair like I did in the jungle. Let me tell you being run out by John Fashanu is about as bad as life can get. Me, Phil Tufnell, scourge of bowlers the world over, giving my wicket away to Fash the Bash.

I might have been on the other side of the world but I could hear them chuckling in the Middlesex dressing room as Fash's throw left me stranded and my reputation in tatters.

Still, if that's the worst thing that happens in two weeks in a rainforest surrounded by and eating creepy crawlies then the ordeal couldn't have been that bad.

For the people who tuned into it for an hour a night it must have looked as if we were having a right laugh but they didn't see the other 23 hours of the day. If the devil is supposed to make work for idle hands I wish he'd found something for me to do when I was in there. Forget the rats, the dirt and the lack of decent grub — the biggest killer in the jungle was boredom. It was worse than scratching your arse and watching the rain fall at Headingley.

I should be used to keeping myself busy abroad after all the times England made me 12th man but I'm afraid the usual distractions like bars, beaches and casinos were not available, so I had to content myself with a kip, the odd bottle of jungle juice and a giggle with a couple of the other inmates.

Quite a cast they were too. Wozza (Anthony Worral Thompson) and Linda Barker were top drawer, Fash was Fash and everyone else chipped in. Sure there were a few words said between some of the competitors and certain people had their own agendas, but to me it was just like being in a cricket dressing room. Apart from the people applying lip-gloss and mascara and the ballet dancer breaking his foot.

After nearly two decades as a player I'm used to playing silly games, hearing people tell me their life stories and being starving while waiting for the next meal to appear. Fash probably had the same in his time as part of the old Wimbledon Crazy Gang. Everyone was in everyone else's faces so you were bound to get the odd flashpoint and frankly I'm surprised there weren't more.

The old bush tucker trials were a bit unnerving. Waiting for the results of the vote was worse than facing Patrick Patterson with a hangover and it was always a massive relief when I managed to avoid them. I thought I'd cracked it when I got off with one that had me swinging through the air and another when I was on a giant piece of knicker elastic in the swamp. But the Geordie boys, Ant and Dec, got me in the end when they made me eat the sort of bugs I haven't seen since I turned over my mattress in the digs I lived in as a youngster. Talk about leaving a funny taste in your mouth. I had to spend about a fortnight trying to get rid of it in the time-honoured fashion.

A lot of young cricketers could do worse than spend a couple of weeks like that. It certainly makes you realise how lucky you are when you go away with England. On tour everything is done for you short of having your nappy changed, but in the jungle you have to worry about things like gathering logs — not what colour wine to have with your dinner.

As I said at the time I went in there to get my head down for a couple of weeks and have a bit of a laugh so I was gobsmacked when I got through to the last half dozen let alone when I won the thing. But it was good to be bracketed with Gatt and Beefy on the short list of English cricketers to go and win something in Australia. (And I certainly got more runs than usual). Even if it did mean stepping into Tony Blackburn's shoes and not Derek Underwood's.

I was even more gobsmacked when we arrived back at Heathrow Airport, the place was full of snappers and my ugly mug was all over the papers. I was even chased out of Lord's by a load of schoolkids when I went to have a look at England playing the Zimbabweans. It was the first time anyone there had been pleased to see me and a complete shock to the system. At least when the lads won that Test match on the Saturday the papers starting talking about the lads rather than the scrawny left-armer eating moths in the jungle. Me Phil Tufnell, a celebrity? Get out of here.

Is For...
Kallis
Karim
Keepers
Kenya
King Pair
Kip
Kumble

Kallis

We used to call Jacques Kallis 'Kalahari', as in there's not much there, like the desert, and although he might not have got a handle on our schoolboy humour he can play the game that's for sure.

In 1997 we had him as our overseas player at Middlesex when Greg Blewett got himself picked for the Australian tour party and he did not disappoint. He was absolutely top notch. He is a genuinely quick bowler, a world class batsman and a brilliant fielder. It makes you sick when you run into someone who is so multi-talented, and it doesn't make the old one-trick ponies look too clever in the nets I can tell you.

We should have won the title that year but jumped from ninth in the championship up to fourth and basically most of it was down to Jacques. One NatWest game against Gloucestershire, who were the one-day kings, sticks out. He took four wickets and scored a century which included two reverse swept sixes. Most of the lads could not believe their eyes. If every overseas player was like that you wouldn't mind how many you had in each side.

Karim

Aasif Karim struck a big blow for the ageing left-arm spinners union with his performances in the 2003 World Cup and his performances proved you can dish up some decent twirly stuff even when your age is the same as Thorpey's batting average. Obviously not the fittest bloke in the Kenyan side, he also rammed home the point that you do not have to be Daley Thompson to bowl decently.

He was getting on for 40 years of age at the last World Cup when he had the Aussies tied up in knots, giving them one of their stickiest moments of the tournament. He had taken three wickets before they had even managed to score a run off him. Ricky Ponting, Darren Lehmann and Brad Hogg, who are hardly rabbits, were all back in the hutch, and the veteran tweaker Karim was sitting on figures of three for zip. Ponting, in particular, was done up like a kipper before being pinned by an arm ball — I was back in London at this stage and watching it on the box almost brought a lump to my throat.

Karim reminded me of the old boys you would always come up against in club cricket. Playing on some public park in Hertfordshire, where the outfield is covered in dog turds, your side are cruising at one down for 100, when suddenly a portly old boy starts bowling slow left arm at the openers who can't get him off the square.

Every club has one. The veteran, wearing a pair of big cream flannels whose bowling looks like a candidate for the car park over midwicket, ends up buying the jug after taking five wickets. It just goes to prove there is no substitute for experience at any level.

Keepers

Fact. All wicketkeepers are absolutely barking and make the slow left armers look positively sane with their antics. And it is not just Jack Russell, so out there he once blindfolded a team-mate to stop him finding out where he lived, who is a candidate for the funny farm. Even in pub cricket you can tell the keeper a mile off. They are the chirpy, enthusiatic little buggers who never stop chuntering on to the batsman and the bowlers.

They are always the ones with dirty trousers caused by leaping about unnecessarily for catches just so their bird on the boundary can get a picture of them diving full length to drop another chance. They are almost always neurotic and have little superstitions that make them jump about as if they have got ants in their jockstrap. Some of them will have to touch the bails, the ground and the dangly necklace round their necks before every delivery just to make sure everything is in place.

But as a spin bowler you really notice if the keeper is on his game. They keep the batsman on his toes so he doesn't run too far down the track at you and they even get wickets for you although you wouldn't like to admit it.

At the highest level I wonder how many of Shane Warne's wickets were down to Ian Healy. He could chirrup with the best of them and he and Warnie had quite a double act going with their incessant banter. I remember Mark Butcher going in at number three for England against Australia when Heals was still behind the timbers. Butch had been opening but had dropped one place down the order. Needless to say he was in very quickly, as one of the openers trudged back, and after taking guard he heard Heals say, "It's not much different batting at three is it Butch?" He didn't trouble the scorers and it was another wicket, this time credited to Glenn McGrath on the scorecard, for the glove man.

Kenya

Kenya's performances in the last World Cup were one of the highlights of the tournament and I couldn't believe that people were whinging that they shouldn't have been in the latter stages.

Okay, they got lucky on a couple of occasions. The Kiwis refused to play in Nairobi for security reasons but that was fair enough because the New Zealanders were far too close to meeting their maker after a bomb exploded outside their hotel in Karachi.

Their was also a rumour doing the rounds that the Sri Lankans were feeling the effects of food poisoning a la Gatting and his Indian prawns when they played Kenya — but they were still put away.

Then they had to play Zimbabwe in a do-or-die game and delivered the goods again. Maybe they are a bit away from Test status but they deserved their place at the top table in the one-day game and they certainly gave Australia something to think about which is more than most other sides did. Going further in the tournament than South Africa must have given them a buzz as well.

The Kenyans are absolutely skint but still manage to produce a leggie like Collins Obuya whereas in England, probably the richest board in the world, we can't buy a wrist spinner for love nor money.

The fact that Warwickshire were so eager to get him at Edgbaston proves that there are not many decent leggies around in this country. I can't work that out. We've been trying to find one for at least ten years since Shane Warne first played over here and still nothing.

King Pair

A golden duck in each innings of a match is called a king pair. In my time I have heard the words 'king' and 'pair' uttered by more than one England player as some busty waitress is spotted dishing out the beers in the crowd.

Kip

Everyone knows that my nickname of 'The Cat' had nothing to do with my extraordinary prowess in the field but came about because I could grab a bit of shut-eye anytime, any place, anywhere. If there was a piece of wood six inches wide in the dressing room I could pass out on it even if I was at a day-nighter at the MCG and thousands of Aussies were screaming next to me.

It is very valuable gift. If you like the odd nocturnal adventure — and I have got to hold my hands up to that — then the ability to catch up on your sleep is an absolute lifesaver. There can't be anything wrong in dozing when the cricket is on if the front of the pavilion at Lord's is anything to go by — even if it doesn't always endear you to the skipper.

Kumble

Anil Kumble, or Apple Kumble, as his team-mates at Northampton called him, is not the biggest spinner of the ball in the world but gets more than his share of wickets with his awkward bounce and loopy action.

On one occasion, bowling against England, he forgot the cardinal rule that you don't backchat to a batsman who has just spanked you around. Athers had just reached three figures against the Indians at Trent Bridge when he chirped up that the knock was the worst 100 he had ever seen.

Never one to miss out on having the last word, especially when dealing with bowlers, old Iron Mike came straight back with words to the effect that the ball always seemed to hit the middle of the bat when Kumble had been bowling. A word of advice Apple my old son, keep it shut when the batsmen are on top and only get involved when you've got them tied up in knots.

Is For...
Lamb
Lara
Leg Bye
Leg Spinner
Lehmann
Leveller
Lewis
Long Hop
Loop
Lord's
Lunch

Lamb

Allan Lamb was another larger-than-life character who helped ease me into Test cricket. On the pitch he was a real battler but could also have a laugh at the same time. He famously gave Dickie Bird his mobile phone to hold when he was batting, knowing full well that it would go off.

He was at the centre of the action on and off the pitch. He could arrange anything, had more contacts than a circuit board and was always chirruping into his mobile trying to get something sorted out. He was a one-man social committee on tour and always had plans for a day-off. Golf, barbies, deep sea fishing, Lamby could get you sorted out for anything.

It was no surprise that he moved into event management when he finished playing because on tour he could sort out anything. If you wanted a barbecue on the top of Sydney Harbour Bridge, Lamby would have found a way to get the food and the people up there at the cheapest price and would be the last one to leave.

Lara

For two or three years in the middle nineties the 'Prince of Trinidad' was as good a player as there has ever been. Unfortunately the peak of Brian Charles Lara's career also overlapped with two series against England when in 18 innings he racked up the small matter of 1563 runs at 92.

In the middle of the frenzy was the 375 in Antigua and the only time I have thought I was bowling to someone who had just walked off a spaceship having arrived from a different planet. We never stopped trying to get him out but that day it was inevitable he would break Gary Sobers' Test record score of 365.

All GREAT players have the knack of hitting the ball where the fielders aren't. But not all great players can hit the gap the ball after you have moved the fielder. I think Lara is one of those blokes who, when he looks at the field you have set, looks at the gaps rather than the field. It sounds obvious but you would be surprised how many batsmen there are around who look at the field and not where the scoring opportunities are. The scary thing is that although St John's is not a big ground the outfield was pretty slow and his knock was probably worth 60 more. There are not many batsmen who will murder you wherever you put the ball but Lara was one. Best not to think about it at all.

Gus' face was a picture for the two-and-a-half days we were in the field — whenever he moved a fielder Lara would hit him the ball into the gap. He takes out third slip, move him to gully, Lara cuts him through the gap. Packs the offside, bowls a good length ball on off pole and Lara wafts him through midwicket. Brings in midwicket, bowls a bit straighter, Lara angles him through extra cover. Gus walks back to his mark, looks at me at mid-on raises eyebrows and shrugs shoulders as if to say, "He can't hit my length ball over there!" Just to make him feel better I am absolutely pissing myself and trying not to catch the captain's eye in case I have to turn my arm over.

And so on until Lara has passed Sobers without giving a chance and the outfield resembles the parade at Notting Hill Carnival. Complete with old rastas selling chicken and rice at the spot where third slip should have been. Now you wouldn't get that in St John's Wood.

Then BCL thought he would have a crack at county cricket. Ton followed ton and he topped 2,000 runs with a 501 thrown in. After making five hundreds on the spin he arrived at HQ but we never had a chance to renew our friendship. Lara was going for his sixth straight three figure score and a decent crowd turned up. Gatt won the toss, did the unthinkable and put Warwickshire in. But luckily Richard Johnson sent the crowd home early when he strangled the great man and had him caught down the leg side. And the two most relieved people on the ground were me and Gus. We were still stiff from all the leather chasing in Antigua.

And it wasn't just the English bowling he fancied. The hundreds he got against the Aussies when the chips were down in the series in the Caribbean in 1999 showed that he could cart them as well and his century against South Africa in the World Cup showed there is plenty more where that came from. A good reason for me to leave the scene gracefully I think.

Leg Bye

Leg byes don't count against the bowler's analysis. Thank God for that after all the times I was made to bowl over the wicket into the batsman's pads when we were trying to keep the lid on a game.

Leg Spinner

Leg spinners are all the rage and everyone seems to have one except England. They are the glamour boys of world cricket now when 15 years ago they were virtually extinct. Contrast this with the poor, lonely, sad world of the humble left-arm orthodox spinner. If only I been better with my wrists all those years ago at Southgate I could be a millionaire by now.

Lehmann

Darren Lehmann, who would walk into the England side at the moment, probably as an allrounder, said something that made me think recently.

I was watching the last series between Australia and the West Indies and Lehmann had scored his first Test century. He was interviewed afterwards and said that he had to get a ton otherwise it would be curtains for his international career, and it was only about his tenth Test match.

Think of the Aussies who have won a couple of caps and then been discarded only to come over here and flay our county bowling. As a bowler I find it better not to think about it.

Stuart Law, who is about the best bat on the circuit, played one Test for Australia in 1995 before getting the old red card. Jamie Cox couldn't get a game for them but carts everything around for Somerset and players like Mike Hussey can't even get a look in. It is like England being good enough to leave Mark Butcher or Graham Thorpe out of the side.

Having played cricket at all levels in Australia, from grade stuff to Tests, I know that they treat every game as their last and play as if their lives depend on it. That filters up and you get players like Lehmann, who had just won a World Cup, worrying about their place in the side. The conveyor belt also keeps churning them out, which is slightly worrying for our lads.

Lehmann, though, is not your typical Aussie cricketer you see round the place nowadays. He carries a stomach around with him that would not have seemed out of place in some of the teams of the forties, likes a smoke, a beer and a day at the races yet still does the business when it matters. Look at the way he carried Yorkshire to the title a couple of years back. Just because he doesn't conform to people's stereotype of an athlete doesn't mean he can't turn on the style. My type of player.

Leveller

Of all the team sports, cricket is the biggest leveller. You can be playing in a winning team and still feel crap because you can't take a wicket or you can score a hundred one day and get out for a duck the next day.

In athletics, for instance, Linford Christie would know approximately what time he was going to run the 100 metres in. Short of twanging a hamstring, he was always going to run it in around ten seconds.

Sodding cricket, however, is different. A batsman can be in the form of his life and averaging 100 but only has to nick his first ball and he's back in the pavilion as if he's a tail-end Charlie.

Bowlers have it just as bad. There are times when I have taken one for 100 and deserved, say, three for 60, and there are other days when I've taken five for 30 by bowling a mixture of long-hops and half-volleys which have all gone straight to fielders. When you wake up in the morning you just don't know what sort of day it is going to be.

Lewis

Chris Lewis was one of the most talented players of my time with England but I know he drove some of the coaching staff absolutely bonkers. It is not as if David Lloyd needed any more encouragement to be bonkers but Lewis almost drove him to the edge. At least with me they knew that whatever I had been up to the night before I was always busting my bollocks to win when we actually got onto the pitch. With Lewis, I don't think they were so sure.

After a succession of England captains had tried to get to the bottom of him, Athers thought he would be successful and would turn the enigma into a bowling and batting machine. He was wrong. He was marked down as a wrong 'un by Athers on his first tour as captain when Lewis had a skinhead in the West Indies and promptly ended up going down with sunstroke. As Keith Fletcher, our governor at the time, said in his distinctive voice, "He's gone and had a pool ball, the pwat."

Another time he turned up late at The Oval, which is quite good going for a south London boy, as he was at the time, and claimed he had a punctured tyre. No phone call to the ground or to Athers to say he was going to be late – and all this on the first day of a Test match. You can imagine how impressed Illy was when he found that he had posed naked for a woman's magazine. That would definitely not have happened in his day.

I thought I was the only one with the ability to rub the boss up the wrong way like that. Lewis proved me wrong on that score.

Long Hop

This is the ball the bloke at short leg won't thank you for bowling. Asking one of your mates to field three feet from the bat and them bowling a half-tracker means it's your round for the rest of the season if the poor fellow under the lid survives being hit between the eyes.

Loop

When someone told me I was a bit of a looper I thought they were referring to my colourful past. In fact they were talking about the way I bowled and the fact that I managed to give the ball a bit of air.

Many spinners have made a living out of firing the ball in at

142

leg stump so it is satisfying to be recognised as someone who gave it a bit of flight.

Commentators talk about bowlers having a good loop and that is how you do the batsman in the air. They take a couple of strides down the track, get beaten in the flight so they are nowhere near the ball and the old gloveman whips the bails off. Lovely.

Lord's

The home of cricket and a hell of a place to turn up at for work on a Monday morning, but Lord's cricket ground has seen a lot of changes since I first arrived clad in leopard-skin g-string and winklepickers. The new media centre is the most striking addition and it gives the hacks a great view of the action even if it does look, as someone pointed out when it was opened, like Cherie Blair's mouth.

One thing that has never changed at HQ though is the stewards with their blazers and their snooty attitude.

In 1991, when the squad to go to Australia and play in the World Cup was announced, I was the subject of a bit of press interest. All the papers, and some of the lads' mags, wanted to know about this young spinner, who, horror of horrors, smoked fags, went out occasionally and had been in the odd scrape. Remember, this was a couple of years BW (before Warne).

Anyway a journalist had arranged to meet me to do an interview ahead of the winter trip when I was playing for Middlesex at Lord's. I met the bloke and tried to take him into the pavilion so we could have a chat.

Our route was barred by one of the blazers who stuck up his arm and told us it was members only. I wouldn't have minded except that I was wearing my whites, my Middlesex sweater and a game of cricket was going on out the front so there was a reasonable chance I might have been a player. He obviously wasn't that impressed.

I pointed to the badge on my sweater and introduced myself. I don't want to blow my own trumpet but I was the spinner with the most wickets in the country that year and had just had my champagne moment against the West Indies at The Oval. So when I said "Phil Tufnell, and this bloke's from the papers" you would have thought it would have registered somewhere.

His brain went through the gears and eventually we were let in as long as we sat outside. I have never gone in for the big-time Charlie — don't you know who I am approach — but he should have recognised someone who had been playing there for more than five years and going through the gates every day. Where do they get them from?

Still I'm in good company. Sunil Gavaskar was knocked back once when the bloke on the gate informed him he was the fifth Indian that day who had claimed he was Sunil Gavaskar and Nasser Hussain was also stopped from going in once. And he was England captain at the time. It beggars belief.

Another time, during the 1999 World Cup, Bumble was putting the England team, who were about to play Sri Lanka, through their paces on the outfield. Another one of these stewards wandered up and asked if he had permission to throw balls at stumps on the outfield. At the so-called home of cricket. No wonder we didn't get past the first stage.

Lunch

A career in any game that stops for meal breaks has got to be worthwhile, but the days of Gus wolfing down plates and plates of roast beef have long gone. Players now munch on cereal bars and give you a funny look if you ask them to pass you the salt.

Nancy, who looked after the players' meals at Lord's, got her MBE presented to her in the Long Room. They should have made her a baroness.

She was interviewed by *Wisden* a few years back and very loyally said that none of the players had ever asked her for a hangover cure. For someone whose bacon butties made me human when my head felt like I'd been attacked with a shovel that was pretty good of her.

Her lunches were legendary and although they would not have been on the menu at The Ivy they were just the sort of stuff a cricketer needed to keep going. No wonder Gatt never moved counties. Don't forget that many of the younger lads were reliant on Nancy's catering to keep loaded up. If she hadn't looked after us most of the Middlesex squad would have gone down with scurvy.

Is For...
Malcolm
Maynard
McGrath
Melbourne
Michelle
Middlesex
Muppet
Muralitharan

Malcolm

Big Dev is another who passed 1,000 wickets recently but his batting made me look like Brian Lara. We didn't actually play that much Test cricket together, but when we did play in the same team I am pleased to report that I generally got the better of the argument about who was going to be batting at number 11.

However, with a ball in his hand he could bowl as quickly as anybody else around, and was no slouch even after his 40th birthday. He really put the wind up some of the best batsmen in the world but a combination of mismanagement and injuries meant we did not see the best of him in English colours.

Maynard

Matthew Maynard is another legend on the circuit and a top boy. When I started out I loved the trips down to Wales to play Glamorgan before going out on the sauce with Maynard. They drink something called Brains SA down there and I think the SA is short for skull attack. It felt like that some mornings when I was attempting to bowl at him. They even used to call him Ollie after Oliver Reed for his ability to sink the juice and then perform the next day.

He is a cult hero to the Taffs and still a hell of a player but after the 1994 trip to the Caribbean he never really had a look in at England level. He should have done.

McGrath

If you met Glenn McGrath away from a cricket pitch you wouldn't mark him down as one of the most ruthless bowlers in the business unless you were one of those wild pigs he likes shooting. Put a ball in his hand though and he turns into one mean hombre and probably the world's top sledger.

He couldn't get through to Alan Mullally once though. His only response to some of the harshest verbals ever dished out on a cricket pitch was to smile back. With Big Al's Australian background you can imagine the sort of stick he was getting.

McGrath has a habit of identifying the prime danger man

in a side and then dissecting them like a surgeon would. In recent years he has marked out Brian Lara, Sourav Ganguly and Athers for special attention and has reaped the rewards. With Athers it seemed he only had to run-up to get him out so that marks him out as a special bowler.

Not the world's best batsman though and I was relieved to retire from the first-class game with a higher average than Mr McGrath although I never brought up our respective batting abilities when I was at the crease and he had a ball in his hand.

On the last Ashes tour over here, one of his team-mates Colin 'Funky' Miller said that if McGrath could outscore him in any of the early tour games then Miller would take up residence at the bottom of the order.

This is a ploy someone should have used on me. When they were batting together in one early game they were trading blows and McGrath got up to the high 30s before he was dismissed. If someone like Chris Lewis had offered me the same challenge I might be classed as an allrounder by now.

Melbourne

The Melbourne Cricket Ground is one hell of a place to make your Test debut. Nothing I had seen while playing in front of one man and his dog had prepared me for it. Everyone says it is a massive step up to Test cricket but this place is unlike anything to be found in leafy North London.

I had seen Lord's on a Test match Saturday, with its heaving crowds, while doing my stint on the groundstaff, but the MCG holds four times as many punters as HQ. And it is Boxing Day, and the spectators are topping up the booze levels from the day before, and it is packed, and they are all Aussies. Oh shit.

In 1959 more than 130,000 people crammed into the ground to listen to the American preacher Billy Graham. There were not quite that many inside to see PCR Tufnell become the 547th man to pull an England cricket jumper over his head but it felt like it. It is safe to say I was crapping myself. Especially with local hero Dean Jones trying to knock my block off by battering the ball back at my bonce when I came on to bowl.

The crowd loved Jones, took an immediate dislike to me, and watched like spectators at the Coliseum as Dino tried to butcher my Test career. I got away unscathed, just. But I did not endear myself to the nuts in the stand during a World Series game later that winter.

We had had a dismal time in the triangular series but were still in with a chance of pipping New Zealand to the final on run-rate if we could beat the Aussies. Set 223 to win, I arrived at the crease with nine down and 176 on the board. I was serenaded all the way to the wicket by an appreciative crowd singing "Tufnell is a wanker" and when I joined Gus in the middle I was pissing myself. I could hardly see the ball for the tears as the big man and I set about the bowling to get us up to 219 for nine with one ball left. My contribution was a magnificent five, while Gus had nurdled and nudged his way to 38 not out, but crucially for England's hopes I had the strike.

At the other end Goochie's nemesis Terry Alderman pawed the ground nervously knowing that if he was hit for four off the final ball of the game by Tufnell he would never live it down. My back foot drive through extra cover was perfectly executed but the ball went through undamaged to Ian Healy and we were on our way out of Melbourne.

Michelle

I love this expression because it proves that the vocabulary of cricket is evolving all the time and the bird in question is double fit. The lady in question is not, as the name might suggest, my latest squeeze, but the woman who played Catwoman in the first Batman movie.

So if you take five wickets in an innings you can claim a Michelle, as in Michelle Pfeiffer, or 'five-for,' I got a funny look off the missus once when one of the lads piped up about five yards away from her, "Do you remember the Michelle you got in Nottingham this year, Cat?" That one took a bit of explaining away.

Middlesex

I couldn't have played for any other county than Middlesex even though I was tapped up by other sides a couple of times. I am a Middlesex boy and a Middlesex supporter therefore I played for Middlesex, simple as that. I was loyal for 18 years as a professional cricketer and had a fantastic time turning out with some great players and, more importantly, some great blokes. We played some pretty decent cricket at times as well. And in return they looked after me when I was in trouble and stood by me through some pretty tough times.

That's why I was so disappointed not to get an extension to my contract. Let's get one thing straight. I didn't retire from cricket to go on a game show. Once I was offered the show Middlesex refused to release me from three weeks of the season and that is fair enough. In professional sport you have to do everything 100 per cent or you will be found out.

But I felt I had at least two or three years left in me playing county cricket although any England ambitions were probably out of the window. You don't retire from cricket over a beer, and the thought had been knocking around in my head for a while that I would have to look at my options if they didn't offer to extend my deal.

I had been badgering the club about an extension for about six months and all they had said was that they would review the situation in the middle of the season. That's brilliant if you're a 19-year-old who's just got his first contract but a 37-year-old needs a little bit more security than that or else he's going to start looking around and wondering what to do. It is not as if I was injury prone or had anything to prove.

I felt I still had a lot to offer the county. Although I was not captain, I was the senior pro once Gus had left a year before and enjoyed passing on some of my experiences to the younger lads and showing them some of the tricks of trade.

I still love playing cricket or else I would have packed it in years ago and I thought I could help the kids out in the same way that Gatt and Embers helped a young Tuffers all those years ago. I was looking forward to putting my back into my bowling and having a real crack at cricket in Division One after busting a gut to win promotion last year.

So after all that time working at the same place it was a bit of a shock to wake up one day and not be going into St John's Wood. Let's face it Lord's is a pretty decent place to go to work and plenty of my Highgate mates would gladly have swapped places with me over the years. They have got a great bunch of lads down at Middlesex and I am sure I'll pop my head in for a cuppa, or something stronger, now and then. But if they need any help or someone to turn their arm over occasionally then they've got my number.

Muppet

Sometimes sledging can you make you laugh, like the time the whole Aussie slip cordon collapsed after Eddo Brandes' comeback to Glenn McGrath's inquiry about why he was so fat (answer, "Because every time I shag your wife she gives me a biscuit"). But sometimes it is just downright abusive.

After taking a few wickets for the Middlesex stiffs I finally got a run with the firsts at New Road against Worcester in 1986.

Beneath all the banter I was quietly shitting myself when I went out to bat at number 11. There were a few creases in my flannels, my shirt was flapping and my helmet was about three sizes too big. It is safe to say my entrance was not on a par with Viv Richards.'

David Smith was fielding at silly point. The same David Smith who was drafted into an England tour of the West Indies because he enjoyed playing fast bowling so much he wore the bruises on his chest as a badge of honour. So on my debut I felt I had a psychopath standing about a yard from me and that did nothing for my first night nerves.

My reputation had obviously not reached New Road and the first thing I heard from Smith was "Who's this f****** muppet."

I nearly fainted with shock. I knew that I was playing with the big boys, and I was not expecting anyone to shake my hand as I walked out, but I didn't anticipate that. I am ashamed to report that it rattled me slightly but I nurdled the ball around against the spinners to make a fearless eight that coupled with nine in the second innings saw my average reach the dizzy heights of eight-and-a-half. It was a battle to keep it there for the next 17 years.

Anyway, after hanging around for a while, I was almost considering myself as an allrounder when Neal Radford started pinging the ball around my ears and I sensibly ran myself out. After that display I was nominated for life membership of the number 11's club.

Muralitharan

The Sri Lankan spinner Muttiah Muralitharan is one of the best bowlers in the world and I confidently expect him to get at least 600 Test wickets. But he has always attracted a bit of controversy.

It is easy to see why he cops a bit of stick — he has a bit of an odd action. But when David Lloyd, the then England coach, pointed this out he was jumped on from a great height very sharply. Murali has a kink in his arm when he bowls but the fault lies in the rules. They say a throw is when the arm is partially or completely straightened. If you get rid of the partially bit of the law then he is in the clear every time and it is happy days all round.

Some of the quicks have a bit of kink in the action when they are bowling at their fastest and this rule change would sort all that out as well. Anyway Murali's been cleared by the ICC and that should be that, so we can concentrate on watching a great craftsman at work and trying to work out how to play the bugger.

One place not to play him is on a raging bunsen. But when England played Sri Lanka in 1998 at The Oval the groundsman dished up a pitch with no grass on it and it turned absolutely square. Some spinners, myself included, seem to struggle when they are presented with a turning wicket because they are expected to roll the oppo over. Murali has no such worries. He got 16 wickets and England got murdered.

You wouldn't want to be a young Sri Lankan spinner trying to copy your hero's action though. It would be impossible for anyone else to bowl like that and kids who tried it would probably end up in the casualty department with their arm in a sling.

Is For...
Naughty extras
Nelson
Nervous Nineties
Nets
New Ball
Next Botham
Nick
Nicknames
Night-watchman
No-balls
Northampton

Naughty extras

I might have given it the streetwise cockney bit on my early tours but secretly I couldn't believe some of the things that were going on. It was a real eye-opener to a shy retiring boy from north London.

In Sri Lanka we were staying in one of the poshest hotels in Colombo but after a day's play some of the boys would slip down the road for a rubdown. I couldn't understand why they didn't just let the team physio sort out their aches and pains and then relax in the plush hotel bar. So I decided to find out for myself.

After bowling 30-odd overs in a dustbowl you need to relax, but this was ridiculous. I tailed one of the boys down the road and saw him enter a massage parlour that, even to my untrained eye, looked like a bit more than a place to go for a quick spot of extra-curricular physio.

The massage I got was one of the most thorough I have enjoyed in nearly two decades as a professional — no disrespect to Dean Conway and Wayne Morton, but they weren't a patch on the women dishing out the treatment in there.

The dark-skinned bird who was seeing to me was definitely a pro in one or two areas and when she asked me if I wanted any extras I quickly realised why all the boys had been hotfooting it to her gaff at stumps. Those are the sort of sundries, as the Aussies call them, I don't mind seeing against my name.

Nelson

Nelson is yet another mysterious figure in cricket. Just as the Australians have their Devil's Number of 87 we have our one little bogey figure in England in 111.

I don't reckon we get any more wickets when the score is 111, or 222 (a double Nelson) but a few times I have been praying that we will get a third or fourth wicket when the opposition have racked up 777.

The umpire David Shepherd is famous for his Nelson routine. When the score gets to Nelson, or any multiple of it, he starts hopping about as if he's got a nasty dose of the clap. He has to have a foot off the ground at all times until the scoreboard turns over and for a burly ex-rugby player like Shep acting like a ballet dancer takes some doing.

Nervous Nineties

The only time I got into the nervous nineties was when my runs conceded figure was getting near to needing another column in it. It is as bad for a bowler to concede a century as it is for a batsman to make a duck, and nearing the landmark would always bring out the worst in me. I would do my best to get taken off by firing the ball in at the leg stump but that would only make the skipper keep me on.

The batsmen would not be able to launch me back over my head but could still milk singles. Even though I was not taking wickets the captain would think I was in control as I was not getting smashed all over the gaff, so more often than not he kept me on.

I have conceded more tons than I care to remember and they usually look OK if there are half a dozen scalps in the wickets column. However one for 174 was a very disappointing way to sign off from Test cricket, even if I didn't know at the time that last orders was going to be called on my international career.

Batsmen do get the jitters in the nineties as well. I think Michael Slater and Steve Waugh have about 20 scores in the nineties between them. As they have got around 15,000 Test runs and 40 tons between them as well it means they couldn't have got nervous too often.

Even Iron Mike Atherton himself, who faced the quicks like he had the nervous system of a jellyfish, succumbed to the odd bout of the collywobbles as he was getting close to three figures.

At Lord's in 1993, he was the only bat in our side who coped with the Australian attack and having seen three of their batsmen make tons (and Mark Waugh 99) he grafted his nuts off for 80 in our first dig.

In our second innings (the Aussies, of course, only batted once) he got his head down again and got up to 97. Then the red mists descended after he pushed the ball away for a comfortable two. He and Gatt looked at each other, knowing that a third run would get Athers to the coveted three figures and set off for the run. Big Merv Hughes had the ball airbound and by the time Ian Healy whipped the bails off Athers was sprawled on the turf as if he if had been chucked out of a pub at closing time. Run out for 99. It's the sort of thing I could only dream about.

For someone who had gone through that sort of trauma, I was a bit surprised when he let Alec Stewart biff the South African bowling around at Trent Bridge only to be left stranded on 98 once England had knocked off the winning runs. Apparently Stewie asked him if he wanted to get to a ton and Athers just told him to knock the runs off and win the game. I would have bitten the Gaffer's hand off if he had offered me the chance of a Test hundred.

Nets

I was never a great one for nets. I came very close to meeting my maker when Goochie forced me into the nets once and after that tried to give them a wide berth. There is method in this madness. A lot of the nets in this country are not up to scratch and you are more likely to get injured batting in them against some county second teamer than you are by facing Shaun Pollock in the middle. Look at how many players are injured in the nets rather than on the pitch.

In Australia the nets are usually brilliant and the players they are turning out are pretty handy. For nets to be any use they must replicate the conditions of a match. Too many batsmen pretend they are Viv Richards in practice only to go out and play like Chris Tavare in the middle.

Batsmen are also never out in the nets unless you knock all three poles out. They claim you would never have a fielder wherever they knock the ball in the air and take great glee in trying to smash you over your head.

Bowlers are not much better. During the mid-1990s England had a real no-ball problem until someone realised there was no bowling crease in the nets and the bowlers were delivering the ball from about 20 yards away from the batsman. So in effect the boys were practising how to bowl no-balls. Madness.

New Ball

When the quicks have a new ball in their hands they have the look of Satan himself about them. A cricket ball, as I found out too often for my liking, is hard and when it's new it's like a lump of concrete. The fast bowlers always find a yard or two of extra pace when they have the new conker in their hand and the times when I went out to face the second new ball were very hairy indeed. Even with the amount of padding available nowadays a clunk with a hard ball bowled at 95 miles an hour can leave you looking like you've done a few rounds with Lennox Lewis. A black eye does little for your credentials with the ladies either.

It might be five o'clock, and they may have bowled 25 overs in the day, but they get a gleam in their eye with a brand new cherry at their disposal. I don't mind admitting that, as Alex Ferguson described the latter stages of a close Premiership title race, it is a buttock-clenching moment as you contemplate your likely visit to the nearest accident and emergency department.

Fortunately the new ball flies off the bat just as quickly as it comes on and you have no trouble picking out a fielder so you can save your skin and get back into the dressing room without causing yourself too much of an injury. And to think some blokes make a career out of opening the batting.

Next Botham

The Next Botham, like an edge from Brett Lee, has proved hard to catch in the decade or so since the big man's retirement. It is not a nickname that ever stuck with me despite being a dashing batsman and quick bowler at school before I discovered the delights of the opposite sex. Something had to give and willow wafting was at the front of the queue.

As soon as some poor kid gets three for 50 and 20 runs he is immediately hailed as the Next Botham, and from then on he can't get a run or pitch it on the cut stuff. David Capel, Derek Pringle, Chris Lewis, Darren Gough, Phil DeFreitas, Andy Flintoff, Craig White — the list goes on. Goughie actually looked the best bet when he was hammering the Aussies all around the SCG on his first tour and doing Mark Taylor like a kipper with his slower ball. But one mention of the B-word and, although he could still bowl, he couldn't bat to save his life.

World class allrounders, who would get into a Test side as a bowler or a batsman, do not grow on trees and cricket fans were lucky that in the Beefy era there were a handful of them around — with Imran, Kapil Dev and Richard Hadlee doing their stuff. Before Botham came along England also had a few years of Tony Greig, who was pretty handy with bat and ball, but to find an allrounder worthy of the name before Greig you have to go all the way back to Trevor Bailey.

Cricket followers of my age grew up with Botham and just assumed that another one would be along as soon as he retired — but life's a bitch and it hasn't happened.

We will just have to get used to the idea that the Next Botham does not exist — here or anywhere else in the world although the South Africans may have come closest on the pitch with Jacques Kallis. No-one will get ever get near to him off the pitch.

Nick

I spent most of my career trying to get the batsmen to nick the ball to slip or the keeper. Unfortunately one or two brushes with the law also ended up with me spending a night in the cells to sleep off the effects of a lengthy session.

In Antigua, the prison is next to the St John's Recreation Ground and the inmates sometimes do a bit of maintenance at the ground as part of their rehab.

Thus the strip that you are bowling could have been prepared by a mass murderer or worse. When Brian Lara got his 375 in 1994 at St John's I wondered what I had done wrong to be bowling on a lump of concrete like that. I remember thinking that a couple of days in the adjoining nick would have been preferable to nearly three days having to serve up for Mr Lara.

Nicknames

Most cricketers nicknames are pretty unimaginative such as Thorpey, Tuffers, Athers and Nashy but there are a few gems around. Merv Hughes was also known as 'Fruit Fly' because he was such a pest while Alex Tudor is called 'Bambi', for pretty obvious reasons if you have seen him trying to run in pads.

Michael Bevan, who is the best finisher in one-day cricket, as England know to their cost, is known as 'The Terminator' and Steve Waugh is 'The Iceman' for obvious reasons although 'Tugga' is what the players call him.

Quick bowlers love to have a nickname because it goes with their status as some sort of prize-fighter. Hence Shoaib 'The Rawalpindi Express' Akhtar, Allan 'White Lightning' Donald and Glenn 'The Enforcer' McGrath. Unfortunately for McGrath he is also known by his mates as 'Pigeon' which doesn't have quite the same ring to it.

McGrath got that as a youngster with New South Wales where they reckoned there was a pigeon flying non-stop around the world which couldn't land because McGrath had nicked his legs.

Spinners don't fare as well as the quick boys. Apart from yours truly 'The Cat' and Warnie, also known as 'Hollywood', the best around is the 'Turbanator' which belongs to the Indian twirler Harbhajan Singh.

Colin Miller the former Australian off-spinner was also known as 'Funky,' He was well known for turning up at games with his hair dyed to suit the occasion. He turned up to play on Australia Day with it coloured yellow and once played a Test match with a blue barnet.

This slightly eccentric behaviour was not the reason behind his nickname. He has a CD which he used to play to relax himself before games. It was the Tone Loc song 'Funky Cold Medina' played 12 times at different speeds. It did its job. Miller was one of the most laid-back players I ever ran into.

Night-watchman

I spent a lot of years trying to get birds past the night-watchman at England team hotels and a few quid in their back bin usually did the trick. However, I was never employed as one myself by any team I played for. The poor sod who picks the short straw and has to do night-watchman duties has my deepest sympathy. The whole thing is a nonsense.

There are eight overs left to be bowled in the day and the West Indies quicks have you at, say, 10 for two. So who is the best bloke to go in and bat for the rest of the day? A number ten who bowls medium-pace dobbers for a living or the number five who actually gets paid for batting? It is, as our friends down under would put it, a no-brainer.

As I think I may have said before it is a batsman's game and this proves it. Not content with having most things in their favour, (rules, equipment and so on) they also want the bowlers to go out and blunt the new ball for them when the light is getting a bit iffy so they can protect their wicket for the next day.

Australia have knocked the idea on the head saying that if you are paid to bat then you go in before the blokes who are paid to bowl. And quite right too, it's a dangerous enough game as it is.

No-balls

I managed to bowl four no-balls in the first over of a spell against Essex once, which predictably went down like a sack of the proverbial with the skipper. Spinners are never supposed to overstep the crease and when they do they usually get slammed by the blokes in the commentary box — mostly batsmen and ex-fast bowlers funnily enough. I know that it is a hanging offence and you are gifting the opposition extra runs but you'd think they never bowled a no-ball in their illustrious careers.

A no-balling controversy reared its head when England played Pakistan a couple of years ago and TV replays showed that several batsmen were given out when the bowlers had clearly overstepped the crease.

David Shepherd was one of the umpires at Old Trafford at the time and I know he was on the verge of retiring from the game when he saw the highlights. Saqlain Mushtaq, in particular, had clearly gone over the white line when he got out Ian Ward, Andy Caddick and Dominic Cork.

It can't be beyond the wit of the authorities to get some sort of gizmo installed to help the umpires out on things like this. They had enough to do at that stage of the Test match with the way it was going and help with dodgy no-balls would not diminish their status. Mind you the whole thing deflected the attention rather nicely away from England chucking a game away that they should have won.

Northampton

Going to bowl at places like Wantage Road in Northampton makes you think you have chosen the wrong profession. It is one of the flattest tracks around and to be honest I would have fancied my chances of getting that elusive first class hundred on it if the batsmen had ever given me a look-in.

Their football team is called the Cobblers and frankly bowling on it was a load of the same.

Is For...
Olonga
One-cap Wonders
On-the-one
Over
Overseas Players
Over The Top
Over The Wicket

Olonga

Apparently Henry Olonga, the former Zimbabwean quick bowler, fancies himself as a bit of a crooner and has a career as an opera singer ahead of him. If getting up in front of hundreds of people and singing something from 'Madam Butterfly' takes balls it is nothing compared to the stand he took against Robert Mugabe's regime when the last World Cup was in full swing.

While England were dithering about whether to go to Harare to play a game of cricket and then squabbling over lost points and the financial repercussions, Olonga literally put his head on the block by wearing a black armband in Zimbo's opening match.

His gesture, and that of Andy Flower, was one of the ballsiest, bravest things I have ever seen in a sports arena. At the time Olonga had most of his career to look forward to, travelling the world, playing cricket and enjoying a life that millions of Zimbabweans can only dream of.

But when he thought that enough was enough, and he could use his high profile as a lever to protest against the rulers of his country he had no hesitation in using it. His actions spoke far more than the million words of bullshit spouted by the English cricket authorities.

He had everything to lose and as a young, black player no-one was really surprised when he was left out of the side later in the tournament. According to Flower, the Zimbabwean authorities even made him pay his own hotel bill — he is probably better off without them.

People talk about courage in sportsmen but it often doesn't amount to more than being struck on the chest by a short one or holding your nerve at the end of a tight one-dayer.

Olonga's actions could have seem him trying to dodge bullets instead of cricket balls or, even worse, his family being targeted by Mugabe's bully boys. He didn't duck the issue and did what he thought was right and you can only take your hat off to a brave bloke.

Why didn't England think of doing something like that instead of fudging the issue?

One-cap Wonders

After my first Test in Melbourne I thought I would be applying for membership of the one-cap wonders club but thankfully I got up to two pretty sharpish. Although I have heard that one or two of them meet up occasionally to mull over their Test careers over a few beers, so it must have its compensations.

But it is a pretty sobering thought that the most common number of caps for an England player to have won is one. All your life you dream about playing for England but one bad game, argument or injury and you're red-carded permanently.

Tony Pigott just happened to be in New Zealand in the eighties when all of the England quicks were injured. He was tapped up to play, cancelled his wedding so he could be there, and took two for 75. Next thing he knows it's "thanks a lot, Tony. You can go now." Must do wonders for your confidence and I bet the future Mrs Pigott wasn't that chuffed either at having her big day moved. She must have had a headache for weeks after all that upheaval.

Mark Butcher's dad Alan is also a member of the club. He opened the batting against India in 1979 for one match but didn't get picked for that winter's Ashes tour. Ned Larkins did, and Butch senior was stuck on one cap for the rest of his life. I bet he copped some flak when Butch Jnr got his second start.

If there are a few hard luck stories in the list of one-cap winners then Alan Wells wins the prize hands down for taking it on the chin. He should have played Test cricket years before he got his first, and as it turned out only, chance to show what he could do.

He had played 15 years of county cricket and the first ball he received at international level ended up in the hands of short leg after hitting his bat. Just think of the number of times he had imagined cover driving his first ball in Test cricket for four or swivelling and guiding it to the boundary like David Gower.

He must have known there and then that, after waiting all that time, his Test career was finished before it started. But when he walked off the pitch with his cricketing life in tatters he smiled. What a guy.

On-the-one

I always used to get a sick feeling in the pit of my stomach when I conceded runs, so to see fielders who were supposed to 'be on-the-one' let the batsmen scamper through for a single used to make me retch. Sorry lads but it doesn't end up in your figures does it?

The boys who are stationed 'on-the-one' are in the ring about 30 yards from the bat and are there to stop the bats taking cheeky singles. If you have a batsman tied up in knots then he obviously wants to get away from the strike as quickly as possible and take the bowling from the other end.

A fielder letting one through his legs just takes the pressure off the batsman and gets him down to the non-striker's end to collect his thoughts and have a breather. I might have my critics in the field, and pots and kettles and all that, but this used to really get my goat. Just-the-one is a different matter altogether and virtually impossible to achieve. Going for just-the-one beer after a sweaty day of leather-chasing is always going to turn into a long evening in the boozer.

Over

One bad over can ruin your figures and make your work for the day look completely worthless. Bowling as tight as a nun's chuff is no good to anyone if your one for 60 from 40-odd overs is turned into one for 90 from 41.

In one-day cricket it is even worse because you don't get the chance to claw back the runs. One bad set of six, your figures are ruined and you are first for the chop next time out.

Given his impact over the years, particularly in the shortened form of the game, it is hardly surprising that Sanath Jayasuriya tops the list for most runs off an over in a one-dayer.

He once smashed Chris Harris of New Zealand for four successive sixes, then lost his form and hit the last two balls of the over for a mere four and a two. That must have been a relief for Harris who would have thought he was on the way to joining Malcolm Nash as one of the bowlers to have given up 36 runs in an over.

In Australia they used to bowl eight-ball overs, even in Ashes series. Can you imagine the damage old Jayasuriya could do to someone's analysis with an extra two balls to smash away? I'm glad I wasn't around then. It was as much as I could do to get to the wicket six times in that heat without collapsing.

Overseas Players

Many years ago, when counties were allowed two overseas players, the cream of world cricket came to play in the English domestic game. You could see Barry and Viv Richards, Joel Garner, Mike Proctor, Imran Khan and Gordon Greenidge giving it some welly every day of the week at places like Hove and Taunton.

The second overseas player is now back in English cricket, and the counties were quick to snap an extra foreigner. There was a lot of bleating with people saying that they would hold back the development of the English youngsters but, frankly, that is bollocks.

With the international calendar virtually taking the real cream of the foreign players out of circulation what was left on the shelves would not have given the overseas boys of the late 1970s and early 1980s too many sleepless nights.

Sure it's great when genuine legends are playing domestic cricket in England. Young kids can learn from them and aspire to be like them but the fact of the matter is that they are not around for the whole season now and we have to take players from the B-list. Two overseas players, with one or two others on moody EC passports, leaves plenty of room for the kids to try and force their way into the side.

Frankly if you can't get one of the eight or nine spots left remaining in the county first XI then you're no good to me as a Test player.

Over the Top

Batsmen love hitting spinners over the top and to be honest I used to want batsmen to try and hit me back over my head for six. When I was a kid I remember watching Bishan Bedi, the old Indian spinner, clapping a batsman after he had been hit for a massive maximum. I thought he was off his rocker until I started bowling. Generally batsmen are greedy bastards and if they hit a six they don't need too much encouragement to have another go at the spinners. By clapping, Bedi was making sure his prey had a second pop at him, giving him a second chance at getting him out.

There is nothing so depressing as seeing a spinner start his spell with mid-on and mid-off back on the fence. What you are saying to the batsman in effect is "I don't think I'm good enough to get you out but don't want you to hit for me over the top. Help yourself to as many singles as you want to, old chap, but please don't do my figures too much damage." What utter bollocks.

Just because you are a slow bowler doesn't mean you have to be defensive. If you bring mid-on and mid-off up into the ring then it says to the batsman, "Right my old son. If you think you're good and hard enough to hit me straight back over my head you just carry on and have a go."

If he gives you the charge, it takes only a tiny bit of turn and he is as good as gone. He is a prime candidate for a stumping, or he may not get to the pitch of the ball and hit one helpfully up in the air and straight down the throat of one of your astutely placed fielders. Making mugs out of batsmen like that is something I'll definitely miss.

Over the Wicket

As one of the longest standing members of the Slow Left Armers Union (SLAU), I always prefer to bowl round the wicket to right-handers. You bowl to get wickets, normally, and round the wicket is the best route for your cack-handed twirlyman.

But there comes a time when you have to go over the wicket to try and bottle up an end if you're going for a few runs. A couple of years ago when England were touring in the bowlers' graveyard of India, Ashley Giles, a fellow SLAUer, was told by Nasser Hussain to go over the wicket to Sachin Tendulkar and bowl outside his leg stump. I love it when a plan comes together and this worked a treat. The little maestro got so frustrated he charged down the track and got stumped for the first time in his Test career. Quite a scalp for young Gilo I would have thought.

So I was a bit shocked to read the next day that Ted Dexter, surprise, surprise, a former batsman, was on his high horse saying the tactics were against the spirit of the game. Well I'm sorry Ted, but if you're getting twatted all over the shop by someone like Tendulkar you've got to change your point of attack.

What are you supposed to do — keep bowling a full-length outside off stump so he can smash you through the covers?

And can you imagine Nasser Hussain walking up to his bowler and saying "I love watching this bloke bat, so lob him a few gentle half-volleys" or "hasn't he got a great cut shot"?

Do me a favour, the game is about a contest between bat and ball, it is not played solely for the benefit of the willow wielders. Or, I am sorry to say, even the crowd. They pay good money to get into the ground but most cricket followers would appreciate that there comes a time when you can't feed the batsman's favourite shots with dross bowling.

I had to use the same tactic a lot in the West Indies. The seamers could not always control batsmen like Philo Wallace and Brian Lara and there's no shame in that, so Athers would get me on just to stop the innings running away from us. And with Gus at the other end it might not have been pretty but it was pretty effective. It might not look great but you are there to try and win a Test match and victories look a lot better in *Wisden* than defeats. It is not rocket science. Dot balls create pressure and eventually pressure creates wickets — even when you are bowling at a genius like Tendulkar.

Is For...
Pace
Pads
Pakistan
Physical Jerks
Plumb
Pommie
Pre-season
Pull
Put Your Hand Up
Pyjamas

Pace

Medium pace bowlers get heaps of praise when they "take the pace off the ball" in one-dayers and the batsmen find it harder to get the ball away. Like many things in cricket it is not atomic physics. If the ball is bowled slowly, the batsman has to generate the pace to get it to the fence and can't nudge it to the boundary or swing through the line without any force. But why don't they just pick a spinner in the first place if they want someone to bowl slowly?

Pads

Pads are things that batsmen strap on to their legs and use to kick the ball away instead of using their bat like they are supposed to. The West Indian batsman Jimmy Adams used his so well in India once that he was christened 'Jimmy Padams' by the locals, and it is incredibly frustrating trying to bowl to someone like that when they are kicking you away all the time.

Many batsmen try and fool the umpire into thinking that they are playing a shot by tucking the bat behind the pad and booting you away as if they are David Beckham.

If they get hit on the pad outside the line of off-stump not playing a shot they can be out LBW, but if the umpire thinks they are trying to get bat to ball then he won't give them. This con has been going on for years, but as the game of cricket is played for the benefit of batsmen alone maybe we shouldn't be surprised.

The Aussies used to have a theory that Nasser Hussain used schoolboy's pads to reduce the chances of him being given out LBW. The idea being that the umpire would think you were wearing normal pads and when the ball hit you above the knee roll he would be certain it was going over the top of the stumps even though it would be hitting middle peg half-way up. I don't know if it's true. The batsmen never shared the tricks of their trade with me, but if he really did wear smaller pads it is a smart bit of thinking.

I couldn't see the point in wearing smaller pads and always made sure I had as much protection around the old pins as I could strap on. If I could, I would have put on two pairs.

174

Pakistan

I only managed one Test against the Pakistanis, at The Oval in 1992, and didn't exactly cover myself in glory as they steamrollered us by ten wickets.

After Beefy's comments about not even sending his mother-in-law to Pakistan (which was straight out of the Tuffers Book of Diplomacy) it wasn't exactly a tour I was desperate to make. But seeing the boys win in Karachi made me realise how much I would have liked to have a bowl over there, although the licensing laws may have been a problem in some parts of the country.

I wouldn't have fancied batting over there too much though. In Wasim Akram and Waqar Younis they had two of the best purveyors of the old 'Sandshoe Crusher' ever to lace on a pair of bowling boots.

The reason why they were so lethal, apart from bowling at 90 mph, was the fact that they could spear inswinging yorkers towards the batsmen's toes at will. Most of the boys ended up trying to dig the ball out of the crease with their feet somewhere near the square leg umpire.

They could also swing the ball a lot more with the old ball than the new one which caused a bit of a furore, and the writs were flying around faster than the deliveries from Waqar were shattering stumps. But that all seems to have died down a bit now that players from other countries can get the ball to dart about a bit after more than 40 overs. Our own Mr Gough is as good as anyone in the world at swinging the old ball.

As quick bowlers, who have never been the sharpest tacks in the box, have mastered the art of reverse swing the physics of it must be reasonably simple and they are. Just make one side of the ball heavy with sweat or whatever you can lay your hands on and, hey presto, if it is launched at the right angle it starts behaving like a boomerang and ducking all over the place.

As a team the Pakistanis are probably the most naturally talented bunch of players you will ever come across, but their capacity for rowing among themselves gives them a self-destructive streak.

They get through more coaches than Michael Caine and his boys in 'The Italian Job' and change their skipper more often than most players change their batting gloves. Apparently Wasim and Waqar only speak to each other when they have to and then it is done via their legal representatives. What a way to run a cricket team. Can you imagine what they would be like if they all pulled in one direction? You wouldn't be able to touch them.

Their schizophrenia was summed up neatly in the 1999 World Cup. In the semi-final they were set 242 to win by New Zealand and bulldozed them by nine wickets. Four days later in the final at Lord's they played as if they couldn't be arsed to turn up and the match was over with about 30 overs left.

Unfortunately for the players their fans are as passionate about the game as the Indians are. Effigies of Wasim Akram have been burned in Pakistan and players have had their houses burned and stoned. Death threats are not unknown either.

It makes losing a championship game with Middlesex and occasionally getting barracked by a bloke who's had a skinful of lager and too much sun look a bit tame in comparison.

Physical Jerks

These days warming up, and even warming down, is a very serious business. When I started out the only reason to get to the ground before 10.30 was to get a fry-up down your neck.

Now you are at the ground at 8.30, do a few laps of the ground, play frisbee football, some fielding practice, some five-a-side footy and a bit of stretching. No wonder the opening bowlers can't do more than five over stints at the start of the day — they are absolutely knackered. Poor old Gus looked like he'd bowled 30 overs uphill into the wind before he'd marked out his run-up for the first time.

At least I used to have a bit of time to recover — the spinners never get on until the traditional last over before lunch when it is two minutes to one and everyone's starving.

And at the end of play, instead of grabbing a couple of beers in the opposition dressing room, you have another run round the pitch and you don't get out of the ground until past eight. On tour you might do the warm down at the ground before being bussed back to the hotel for a swim and it plays havoc with your social life.

But my unique training schedule must be good for something. On the 1994-5 Ashes tour there were only four players available for every match. The two grey beards Gooch and Gatting, keeper Steve Rhodes and PCR Tufnell. Everybody else in the party was crocked at some stage. So I must have been doing something right or was it my fabled 'natural fitness'?

You can take it too far, though, and there have been instances of players getting crocked in the warm-up. Mark Butcher, who was having a terrible run in Australia in 1998-99, had his face rearranged after a collision with Peter Such during a warm-up.

It must have knocked something back into place because Butch, who could not buy a run at that stage of the trip, got a ton in the first Test at Brisbane.

Plumb

A batsman is plumb LBW according to most bowlers if the ball hits him on the pads when they are anywhere in the vicinity of the stumps. I reckon I would have been approaching 2,000 first class victims if all the ones I thought were plumb had been given, but you have to take the rough with the smooth.

Pommie

A term of affection used by our cousins from down under to describe the English. Usually followed by the word 'bastard' as in "If I get you a violin we'll see if you can play that you Pommie bastard."

Pre-season

One of the advantages of going on an England tour in the winter is that you do keep some kind of baseline fitness going, so when you turn up at your club's pre-season sessions you don't look too stupid. Even on the most beery England trips you manage to keep yourself reasonably in trim even if you are sinking bottles of Carib every night. But if you haven't been away on England duty, or worse if you've been on a beano abroad without doing a couple of sessions in the gym, then pre-season training is no fun at all.

At Middlesex we used to have fitness testing up at Finchley once a week from about February for the boys who were in England, and that stepped up throughout the spring. After four or five months stuck in the public bar at the Surrey Tavern it is no surprise that I felt a little green on my first day back.

Gradually you get fit enough to bowl six balls in a row without puking up and as the season approaches you are like a highly coiled spring ready to burst into the action. Well that's the theory anyway. That's what pissed me off about my last pre-season as a pro cricketer at Middlesex. I did all the hard work getting rid of a winter of excess and then packed it in the week before the first-class season started. At least it tuned me up for a spell in the jungle.

Pull

If I had practised my pulling in cricket as often as I practised it off the pitch then I would have batted a lot higher in the order than I ever did.

Put Your Hand Up

I'm pretty sure the Aussies started this one as well but it is used all over the world now by teams who are staring down the barrel of a massive defeat. Thus it has been uttered by more than one captain playing a Test series downunder.

For example you may need 450 to save the match, be four down and have nearly two days to bat. Your captain will then rally his troops by telling the press that, "This game isn't dead. Someone is going to have to put their hand up and dig in."

"Come to the party" is another phrase the coaches love. After one of Gus's heroic stints in the Caribbean when he rolled over eight West Indian batsmen Bumble, our coach at the time, said, "Gus really came to the party when we needed him."

When your skipper says that he wants someone to "Put their hand up AND come to the party" you are really in strife and need to put a call into Mr Botham. One of the few people in cricket history good enough to have done both.

Pyjamas

When I was given my kit as we headed out to the World Cup I couldn't believe my eyes. It was the first World Cup to be played with coloured clothing and England's pyjamas were a rather lovely shade of light blue.

It really didn't feel right going out to represent your country looking like you should be shuffling up the stairs with a mug of cocoa in your hands, but everyone else was wearing them so we had to do the same. The loose tops on the trousers also meant that one or two of our meatier players could get their strides on without getting a hernia.

As our one-day kit has got better though, it is now a nifty dark blue and red number, so our form in the shortened game has gone to sleep.

Although the clothes may be ridiculous, one-day cricket has had a positive effect on the longer game. It might seem like going for a hamburger when you're used to eating fillet steak, but there's no doubt that fielding and running between the wickets are on a different level to where they were even ten years ago. My work on the fence was definitely sharpened up by all the limited overs stuff and, while I was never going to replace Ricky Ponting just backward of square, I could do a job and hold my catches.

All of these skills are useful in the Test arena as well so we shouldn't get too stuck up about the one-day game.

In 2002, England, India and Sri Lanka played a triangular tournament in England and the two matches between England and India at Lord's served up some of the most exciting cricket you will ever see. In front of a packed house, Nasser Hussain made a century and some gestures to the press box saying that he was England's best number three and Banger Trescothick weighed in with 109.

India got the runs after being five down for 150-odd and all bets were off as their fanatical fans invaded the pitch and Sourav Ganguly waved his shirt round his head like Freddie Flintoff had in India. If the pyjama game can produce finishes, and, let's face it, gate receipts, like that we shouldn't knock it.

**Is For...
Queen
Queensland
Queen's Park Oval**

Queen

It is a tradition that the Queen turns up at Lord's during the Test match and is presented to the players at the tea interval. After playing for England for more than ten years and more than 40 times you would have thought I would have played more than three Test matches at HQ. It was my home ground after all and a bit of local knowledge can do you the power of good, especially with the slope that runs across the ground.

I'd hate to think that the powers-that-be were worried I would embarrass them in front of the monarch, or that I'd offer her a fag.

Queensland

I have been to many inhospitable places in Queensland, most notably the fine-leg boundary at the GABBA in Brisbane, and lived to tell the tale. From memory it was always baking hot down there and although the crowds could get a bit lively the sunshine and cold beers more than made up for it.

So when I tipped up in the Sunshine State for a spot of R & R before embarking on two weeks in the jungle for 'I'm a Celebrity' I was bit put out to see the rain teeming down from grey skies. Then it dawned on me. I am used to playing cricket in November when the thermometer is always up around the three-figure mark. When we flew out to do our Dr Livingstone impressions it was the Aussie autumn and we were staying near a rainforest. The penny dropped good and proper then that I wasn't there on holiday. Still you live and learn.

Queen's Park Oval

Queen's Park Oval might share its name with a place in north-west London more famous for a video starring Cliff Richard and The Young Ones but the two places could not be more different. For starters you don't see many half-naked models cavorting around and swigging rum from the bottle in one of Uncle Cliff's videos.

I had a couple of bad experiences playing for England in Trinidad at the ground, notably the 46 all out, which was a shocker for me. And I was on the bench.

Despite these nightmares, it remains one of the best cricket grounds in the world to visit and the crowd is a major factor. About 30,000 punters can get in at the moment, making it the biggest ground in the Caribbean, but come the next World Cup there will be a few more and the place will be absolutely jumping. Especially if local hero Brian Lara is smashing it to all parts of the ground.

When the Barmy Army get their own stand at Lord's I will turn to religion but in Trinidad there is an area called the Trini Posse Stand. The Trini Posse are a bunch of nutters who follow the Windies all over the Caribbean, and the way their side has gone off the boil since the days of Curtly and Courtney that takes some doing.

The Trini Posse Stand is at square leg and has room for about 600 raving lunatics who pay an all-in price for the 'ultimate lime,' 'Liming' is Caribbean speak for drinking, relaxing and generally kicking back.

For about 20 quid you can eat, drink, enjoy the company of dancing girls and watch the cricket all day. When I have watched deliveries of mine fall into the lap of some West Indian lovely jigging around in the stand I have often wanted to swap places with some of the blokes in there.

At the end of the day the stand looks like a camp-site at the Glastonbury Festival with empty bottles, chicken bones and bodies all over the shop. The whole thing was started by a dentist who wanted to up the interest in Test cricket about ten years ago. You wouldn't want to visit his surgery the day after a five-day match.

The ground also stages international cycling and, as you would expect, has a cycling track round it. This sloping bit of concrete does the ball no end of damage when you've been twatted over the fence but is as good a place as any for the Barmies to top up their tans and sup a few rum-and-cokes. With the nightmares England have had on the ground they need all the anaesthetic they can get.

Is For...
Rabbit
Rain
Raise the Bat
Ramps
Reverse Swing
Room-mates
Running On The Pitch

Rabbit

What you get from the missus when you come back from another triumphant tour with nothing to show for it apart from sunburn and a tropical disease.

Rain

Rain is part and parcel of playing cricket in England and it is just something you have to get used to. You can guarantee that if it has been sunny throughout March and April the heavens will open as soon as the first game of the season is underway.

It has come to my rescue more than once after a night out though. It sounds unprofessional, but there is nothing like turning up to a ground with a stinking hangover to see the covers on and the rain belting down.

It gives you time for a couple of hours kip in the dressing room to get your head together while avoiding your captain who will be looking for someone to bowl at him in the indoor school.

Raise the Bat

Batsmen raise the bat when they get to a landmark and the action can vary between the point to the dressing room (Australian batsman getting to 50) to the full axe-swing above their head (Darren Gough getting to 50) but bowlers never had any way of celebrating a personal milestone.

Until the Aussies thought of one. They are so big on the team ethic that they never want anyone to be left out. They were the first team to have the numbers showing where they came in the line of players to represent their country sewn under the badges and they all wear the old baggy green cap for the first session of a game.

It had to be the Aussies who came up with some way for the bowlers to celebrate getting a Michelle or their fifth wicket. When one of them gets a fifth wicket he holds the ball up to the crowd and takes the applause, as if he is a batsman. And why not — if you have slogged through 30 or 40 overs it is nice to get a pat on the back from the rest of the lads. So hats off to them for striking a blow back for the foot soldiers.

Ramps

Mark Ramprakash was the third member of the bat pack, with Nasser Hussain and Graham Thorpe the other two, and had a massive talent for butchering bowling. So we were a bit miffed at Middlesex when he went south of the river to go and play for Surrey of all people. Still he ended up with a championship medal and another Test hundred, so the move must have done something for him.

Like Nasser, he has a bit of a temper if things don't go exactly to plan and I'm afraid his career has not always panned out the way he would have wanted. At county level he is absolutely out of this world, and smashes the bowling all over the shop. I must admit I wasn't looking forward to bowling to him at The Oval after Middlesex won promotion at the end of the 2002 season. Perhaps that was in the back of my mind when I called it a day. He has got every shot in the book but used to become very intense and inhibited when he played for England.

It took him about six years to get his first hundred for England and when he did I thought the old floodgates would open and hurry his Test average up to near 40, but they didn't.

I was so pleased for him when he kicked down that barrier because he had been a team-mate since we were kids. He scored that hundred in Barbados and everything in the garden was rosy but it hadn't been earlier in the tour. When he was left out for one of the games he went loopy and slammed the dressing room door so hard it nearly came off its hinges.

He has won plenty of England caps over the years and people carp that he has been given enough chances to do the business. But if you look at his career he has never really had a decent trot in the side. He is someone who has a very fragile self-confidence. He needs people to boost his confidence — not kick him in the bollocks all the time.

He is a very quiet bloke and a top man, but he managed to get himself tagged early in his career as someone who's a bit feisty and a bit of a loner. Sounds familiar doesn't it?

His desperation to succeed saw him tighten up at Test level and he has never done himself justice internationally although he has managed to average over 40 against the Aussies which takes some doing and I know that they rate him pretty highly.

When I went through one of my numerous sticky patches a few years ago I decided it was because I was too worried about people's perception of me rather than concentrating on my batting. Ramps should loosen up a bit and it would be no surprise to see him come good.

He also had to put up with being my batting coach. On one tour each batsman had to pair off with a tailender to give them the benefit of their experience in the vain hope that the lower order would contribute a few runs.

I am afraid our sessions wouldn't have done anything for Ramps' mental state and I used to drive him barmy as he tried to make me get in line. Now I've retired he can concentrate on his own game.

Reverse Swing

I know a few quick bowlers who swing both ways but when the phenomenon of reverse swing reared its head through the exploits of Wasim Akram and Waqar Younis I thought it could be the end of the twirlymen for good.

As a spinner it was taken as read that you would be turning your arm over when the ball was 50 or 60 overs old. But these blokes started swinging it then and I thought it was curtains. Thankfully the slow men have survived.

Room-mates

Not even facing Ambrose and Walsh on a quick track is as nerve-wracking as the long walk from coach to hotel not knowing who your next room-mate will be. Having to share with someone who has strange habits like going to bed before ten o'clock is obviously a no-no.

Non-smokers have to be avoided and fans of room service curry should be given a wide berth. They stink the room out and being kept awake by strange rumblings from the khazi does not help you prepare for bowling at Lara.

The best room-mate ever was Wayne Larkins, aka Ned. On my first England tour to Australia he really opened my eyes about getting ready to play for England and how valuable it was to be well prepared. He was permanently surrounded by a cloud of smoke and a growing pile of bottles or cans. He made the perfect companion for a nervous new boy like me. I would stumble into the room — which resembled a student flat — to be greeted by Ned grinning through the fog and reaching for another tinnie to push in my direction.

By the time we collapsed into bed the room smelled like a pub at closing time and we didn't smell too much better. You always knew who was rooming with him — they were usually shaking and sweating at nets the next day as the effects of a night with Ned came out of their systems.

Sharing with Derek Pringle was a different sort of education. He always had his nose in a book, a sign of things to come as he is now a broadsheet writer, and I always came back from tour with a few new long words.

Everyone knows Jack Russell is barking and being in the same hotel as him let alone the same room is a complete nightmare. The room is turned into a Chinese laundry, with bits of kit all over the place, he washes his jockstrap in the sink, so cleaning your teeth is definitely not an option, and there are half-done paintings all over the place.

Judge (Robin Smith) would keep you awake half the night ducking imaginary bouncers in front of the mirror and shouting "be strong" to himself. He was completely fearless against fast bowling and completely nuts at the same time — I think the two are connected.

Fortunately those days have gone and you can have a decent kip in your room, smoke to your heart's content and raid the mini-bar without getting a rollicking.

In 1996 Lord Maclaurin gained instant cred with the boys by giving us all single rooms in Zimbabwe and it has been the same ever since. Before he changed it only the captain had his own room. Then bliss.

Running On The Pitch

The trick of picking a left-arm seamer is often overlooked by the selectors but if you have got a twirler in your side it is always worth getting one into the starting line-up so that he can rough up the pitch for the spinners.

Alan Mullally might not have been the most destructive left-armer in the business but he certainly got me a few wickets with his discreet follow-through, and Wasim Akram must have helped out the Pakistani twirlers in the past.

Left-arm quicks, like these two boys, can cause enough damage in a couple of overs to make the playing surface look like a battlefield, with a few subtle scrapes of the ground with their sharpened studs as they follow through. They have to be careful because once the umpire rumbles that they are steaming up the pitch by twisting their feet then they will get a warning which is the equivalent of a yellow card. Three of these and you can't bowl for the rest of the innings.

When the slow bowler turns his arm over from the other end, the right-handed batsman will be so wary of the minefield outside his off-stump that he won't try to hit you out of the ground even if you're doing nothing with the ball. It just puts a bit of doubt in their minds and often that is all you need.

Of course it is not just bowlers who scuff up the pitch. Batsmen have been at it since the year dot.

If they have a tasty bowler of virtually any pace they will run in a straight line up and down leaving a line on the pitch that looks like a tractor has been ploughing up and down it.

The umpires are usually alerted to this by the fielding side screaming at the offender who is always wearing filed metal studs instead of his usual rubber moulded ones. And it is supposed to be a gentleman's game. I ask you.

S

Is For...
Seeing it like a Football
Sex
Sky
Sledging
Sleep
Smell the Leather
Speed Gun
Spinners
Stewie
Streakers
Suncream
Sunglasses
Superstitions
Sydney

Seeing it like a Football

You know the bowlers are struggling when the commentators claim that the batsman is "seeing it like a football." It just means he has got his eye in so well the cricket ball appears about ten times bigger than it is in real life. I think that's what it means anyway. When I batted the ball used to look like a very small marble.

Sex

During the last World Cup it was interesting to see the way teams tried to control the sex lives of their players. I was never one to turn down the offer of an evening's gymnastics, even if it was the day before a Test, and some might say that if they went through my figures they could pick out the times when I had enjoyed some female company before bowling.

Most of the sides left their wives and girlfriends at home although the South Africans did get to see their other halves for a couple of days leading up to the tournament. Amazingly the South African board slapped a nookie ban on the team, saying that although they could see the missus she couldn't stay in a player's room. Result — the disgruntled and frustrated Boks missed out on the Super Sixes.

India let the women turn up once they had got into the Super Sixes and the Aussies met up with their better halves in the latter stages of the tournament. They both made it to the final. I think there is a lesson in there somewhere.

Sky

I loved doing the stints as an 'expert' analyst on Sky television and hope to do a lot more now that I've got more time on my hands. Phil Tufnell, TV pundit and respected commentator? With a reputation like mine? Whatever next?

It did give me a chance to prove that I have picked up the odd thing in 18 years on the county circuit and I like to think I surprised a few of the viewers who probably had me marked down as a tactical half-wit.

It might look glamorous with the backdrop of the Sydney

Cricket Ground or Sabina Park but you are actually watching the cricket on a little screen in Sky's studios in Isleworth. Nothing against that particular corner of London but Barbados it ain't, and the hours aren't exactly regular.

When you are watching Tests from New Zealand or Australia you can be working from midnight to eight in the morning which suited my body-clock right down to the ground.

Sometimes, though, even my ability to stay up all night let me down and the presenter and I had to find ways to amuse ourselves to stop the old eyelids from drooping too much when we were off camera.

Simon Lazenby, who has moved on from presenting cricket in the dead of the night and does the rugby now, was my partner in crime. We decided to liven things up by trying to get the name of a vegetable into every phrase we used. Corkers like "The number three spot is a bit of a hot potato" and "he could play this bowling with a courgette" were being bandied around before we got rumbled. It might sound completely childish but it kept us awake for a couple of hours when the cricket was a bit flat.

On a more serious note, and this is not a job application letter, Sky have done more than most to promote cricket in this country. When I was a kid, showing a vague interest in cricket, all we got of the Ashes series down under was a few grainy highlights. Now if you want to you can watch the thing live, or catch extended highlights later in the day.

One little gripe. In the second Test at Port Elizabeth against South Africa a couple of years back we could have done with the pictures from Sky. I bowled at my old mate Jacques Kallis who, as usual, was digging the Boks out of a hole. He was on 12 at the time and was sure I had him caught at slip by Chris Adams.

Grizzly was certain he had taken the catch but the host broadcaster's pictures did not show whether he had for sure. Sky's pictures showed the catch was clean but the third umpire was not allowed to look at it. Kallis was given a life and went on to make 80-odd not out.

I'm not saying it would have made any difference to the

result of the match, which we drew, but it seemed ludicrous that Sky had better pictures on the ground and the third ump couldn't even look at them.

Sledging

Steve Waugh calls sledging "mental disintegration" but the best way to handle the verbals is by ignoring them. The Australians tried to sledge Athers when he first started out but soon gave up when he either ignored them or gave them a clever dick answer back. Some of the stuff that flies about is quite funny actually.

Shane Warne had a running battle with the South African batsman Daryll Cullinan and had a lot of success getting him out after winding him up. It got so bad that the Boks apparently got a psychiatrist in to help Cullinan which only made Warnie give him more stick the next time he came in.

Warnie's opening line was "I've been waiting for you for a long time and I'm going to send you right back to that leather couch." Cullinan was completely spooked and was immediately dropped from the side. Warnie also riled Nasser Hussain so much in a one-dayer by telling him to slog his bowling that Nas got himself into a right two and eight and was bowled trying to hit the leggie out of the ground.

Personally I used to keep quiet. If I turn round to the batsman and tell him he's crap just before he lofts me into the stands for another towering six then who's the one who looks like a prat?

But the people who claim it is a new thing in the game are barking up the wrong tree. It has been around as long as the game has been played. WG Grace was notorious for sledging and Fred Trueman was known to chuck in the odd one-liner and see the occasional batsman off. They are looked on as rascals but the blokes who have a bit of banter now are crucified in the press. International cricket is a bloody tough game and you are bound to get a word or two said in the heat of the moment. If you don't like it you can always turn off the stump mike.

Talking of which, I remember Goughie using the stump

mike to sledge a commentator, which was probably taking it a bit far. The former England bowler-turned pundit Bob Willis had been giving the Yorkie paceman a bit of stick about his attitude so Dazzler decided to give him some back during the next game.

He knelt down to the stumps and asked Big Bob how he would bowl on the wicket. I know he regretted it afterwards but if you're steamed up and a temptation like that is put in front of you how are you expected to react?

Sleep

Being able to get your nut down and have a kip at any time is a very underrated skill but one that, I am pleased to say, I possess in spades. When I was cadging a lift to a county game with one of the boys I would be in the Land of Nod before they let the handbrake off and although it doesn't make you the most popular player in the side it prepares you for the hard work of the day. Batsman always reckon they can play left-arm spin with their eyes closed, so why shouldn't the twirlers have a bit of a snooze now and then?

I mean you can't be expected to do a warm-up, bowl 25 overs and go out on the razzle without the correct amount of shuteye can you? So getting the zzzds in whenever possible is essential if you're going to last as long in the game as I did.

When we went out to the Australian jungle I was determined to use my kipping skills fully and get my head down for a couple of weeks. I'm afraid that's easier said than done when one of the world's most famous ballet dancers, Mr Wayne Sleep, is busting his ankle by jumping up and down on his bunk. As if spending a fortnight in the jungle is not dangerous enough, old Wayne decided he would liven it up by putting on a trampoline exhibition for the cameras. I'm afraid he didn't get much sympathy from the Tufnell corner of the camp, after we had our little run-in and he had a pop at cricketers, so it was left to poor old Fash to ferry him about. He was used as a carthorse, carrying 'Sleepo', as he called him, to the little boys' room and back again in the dark. Rather him than me.

Smell the Leather

Smelling the leather is a familiar sensation for anyone who has ever walked out to bat in the Caribbean. Tailenders like me don't get any leeway out there — they treat you as if you are Robin Smith and bombard you with bouncers that whistle past your nose. Hence the expression "You're gonna smell de leather today Tuffers."

More ominously, sometimes Courtney Walsh would rev up his old sparring partner Curtly Ambrose by telling him to "perform the operation" as if he was some kind of surgeon. Given my attitude to hospitals and needles that one was always a bit worrying to hear.

Speed Gun

The introduction of the speed gun has given Goughie another reason to puff out his chest when he has just hurled one down at about 96 miles an hour, but it could be used more effectively. It was rumoured that when David Lloyd was England coach he tampered with the speed gun when the South Africans were over on tour making Goughie look slower than he was to dent his ego and get him to bowl a bit faster. I don't know if it is true but it would be a brilliant way to put the shits up opposition batsmen.

I think I would use it the other way round. Just crank it up a few notches and suddenly dear old Gussie is bowling at the same speed as Allan Donald as far as the opposition are concerned. And when the other side are bowling you crank it back down so your batsmen don't get sick with fear when their strike bowler is steaming in.

It would dent the macho image of their quicks who would then start tearing their hair out trying to get the dial up to their normal speed and their line and length would go walkabout. The batsmen could then make hay. It's all in the mind anyway. There was a great hullabaloo when Shoaib Akhtar bowled the first 100mph ball. It is forgotten in all the fuss that Nick Knight, who received the missile, calmly nudged it away as if Shoaib was a medium-pace trundler.

Spinners

Now I am an ex-twirler I can bang the drum for the slow merchants without people saying I am trying to get back into the England team. But in all my years in the game the English attitude to spinners never changed.

In Calcutta in 1992 we had three spinners on tour — myself, John Emburey and Ian Salisbury. On a turning track we went in with just the one twirlyman — Salisbury. We lost heavily on that tour but England still hadn't learnt their lesson eight years later.

India were picking Harbhajan Singh and Anil Kumble while we just picked Richard Dawson in the first Test. Daws managed a respectable four wickets but we didn't have a spinner at the other end to support him. Who knows the conditions best out there? And who picks two spinners? If you are not going to play two spinners in a Test match in India when exactly are you going to play them?

The poor old twirler always seems to be the last man into the team, and the first one out.

Stewie

You can't piss on statues according to the Aussies, and in England Alec Stewart is a national monument. Someone once called him 'The Queen Mother of Cricket' and he is the sort of bloke you would want your daughter to bring home with her. He even managed to get a ton in his 100th Test against the West Indies on the Queen Mum's birthday so they are bound to put a statue of him up somewhere sooner or later. Mind you, the way he is going he will probably stiffen up in about 20 years time behind the stumps and they will just leave him there stuck out in the middle with one arm in the air appealing for a caught behind which the batsman has missed by a foot.

Like all legends things are not always they way the seem, however, and you don't last as long in the game as Stewie has done without knowing how to look after numero uno.

All the stuff that was written about him being put upon by England when they asked him to keep and captain, or keep and bat up the order was miles wide of the mark.

It is quite simple. If you are an allrounder there is more than one way to keep yourself in the team — same if you are a wicketkeeper-batsman. Ian Botham used to say that it almost didn't matter if he failed with the bat because he had another chance to get involved with the ball. In other words it is another chance to keep yourself in the team. Same story with the Gaffer. So don't feel sorry for him.

Likewise his retirement from international one-day cricket. If you want to retire, then retire and don't leave the selectors the option of calling you back into the side. If he had been named in the one-day team it would have been the 'Good Old Stewie, helping England out' cobblers again when he should have just retired from one-day cricket full-stop. At least the selectors managed to resist the temptation not to pick him when even Stewie himself admitted he would not be making it to the World Cup in 2007.

Apart from smashing quick bowling all over the shop, his greatest talent is the knack of keeping out of trouble that I wish had rubbed off on me. For instance, when you are cracking away in the bar after a good win and the tequila slammers are flying about then Stewie — being a true pro — will have a couple of halves and then make a hasty exit leaving you to explain away your hangover to the management the next day. That's why he's got about 90 caps more than yours truly.

Alec will have been for a dawn dip in the hotel pool, had a healthy breakfast and will arrive on the team bus looking like an advert for Sanatogen while the boys who did the late shift are trying not to throw up in their sunhats.

I don't think my nocturnal habits and the fact that I did not play once in the Tests when Alec was captain are entirely unconnected either. I'm afraid to say that in our case opposites did not attract. He was always immaculately turned and bristling with energy and I, er, wasn't.

I did play once under him when Goochie missed the Sri Lanka leg of the Elephants tour to the subcontinent but Stewie was obviously not part of the selection panel. He revels in all the sergeant major stuff and I wouldn't fancy doing a bit of square bashing with him in charge, although he probably would.

Stewie was keeping wicket, batting number five, skippering, driving the bus and taking fielding practice during that match and it was so hot that our manager Keith Fletcher claimed Europeans couldn't play in such heat. Only Judgie did himself any justice with a seven-hour hundred and Stewie was still standing behind the stumps as Sanath Jayasuriya finished the game by pulling me into the stand for six. I don't think he was all that chuffed.

Despite the fact, or probably because, he is a half a lager merchant Stewie can still play the game as well as someone half his age. Unbelievably he still likes facing the quicks and on his day he played Ambrose and Walsh as well as anyone has ever done. He even seemed to enjoy the ball whistling round his earholes when at his age he should have his feet up and a cold tinny in his hand. Still it takes all sorts.

Streakers

Old Trafford came close to having its status as Test match ground withdrawn because of the number of people running onto the pitch without a stitch on. Quite right too — they were all blokes who had obviously been on the old Boddingtons all day and were not a patch on Erica Roe who first got me interested in rugby when she got her Bristols out at Twickenham.

If, however, an attractive young female wants to take her clothes off after a few gins and do cartwheels in front of the slip cordon, who am I to argue?

Suncream

The Aussies used to say that the height of optimism was an English batsman putting on suncream, but it is a vital part of the modern cricketer's armoury.

The bowlers don't have much equipment to help them out so they have to make use of anything they can get their hands on. Allan Donald looked more like Sitting Bull than a quick bowler and Shane Warne's lick of cream on his nose made him look like a clown. Anything that can distract a batsman has got to be worthwhile and let's be honest who is going to tell AD he looks a plonker when he's got a hard ball in his hand?

Sunglasses

He might have been one of the greatest cricketers to walk the earth, but Ian Botham's biggest contribution to the game was to make wearing sunglasses on the cricket pitch cool. Club cricketers the world over have kept millions of pairs of bleary eyes from their captain on a Saturday morning, the result of the "just one after work" deteriorating into a full blown session.

The first ones on the scene, as modelled by Beefy in 1991, could hide all the puffiness produced by a night out with the big man himself and had lenses like satellite dishes.

Sunglasses have been refined now and are an essential part of your armoury – you can even get light enhancing glasses for when it gets a bit gloomy.

We took a bit of stick from the old-timers for the shades but they help with the skiers when you are stranded in the deep all day. Good for a spot of discreet lechery on the beach or in the outfield as well.

Superstitions

If a psychologist spent a summer watching cricket from county dressing rooms around the country the game would quickly lose some of its most influential characters to the asylum. Mature men with years of experience will not leave their seat even if they are bursting for a piss – because if they move an old cricket tradition says a wicket will fall and it will be their fault. Nothing to do with Glenn McGrath steaming in a helpful strip – it is all down to the plonker who got up to have a leak.

It is surprising one wicketkeeper on the circuit has not been pulled up for his habit of walking round the stumps every ball when the spinners are on. He is not auditioning for a part in the next Monty Python film but claims his routine is essential. More than one batsman has accused him of trying to scuff the wicket and threatened him with a slap.

If you ever needed a cunning way to beat South Africa all

you had to do was go into their dressing room lavs and put the seats up. This would reduce one of their leading batsmen to a jibbering wreck and the series we won in 1998 can all be put down to the fact that the England boys made sure the toilets had their lids up.

Steve Waugh always bats with the same red hankie in his pocket, which must be a bit crusty after more than 150 Test matches, while his brother Mark had an interesting thigh pad. He would draw a stick man on the pad every time he scored a hundred and by the time he retired it looked more like a page from a kid's comic than a bit of cricket equipment.

My only superstition when I was batting was to keep my eyes closed at all times.

Sydney

The best place in the world to have a day off. Once you have rolled out of bed it is straight on with the shorts and best wraparound sunglasses. From the hotel it's a quick stroll to Bondi beach, a few Bundaberg rums, an afternoon's malingering and a view that makes Baywatch look like Playschool.

You can spend all day on the beach and not be found by marauding coaches or physios before slipping off for the evening's entertainment — or if you've struck lucky early the afternoon's activities.

Not a bad place to play cricket either especially if you are a spinner. But the fact that Sydney is one of the few pitches in world cricket guaranteed to turn brings its own pressure. You think, "We are on a raging bunsen, this is my manor, I must take wickets." So you end up putting too much pressure on yourself and try to bowl magic balls all the time. It did not help when the part-timer Alan Border took 11 for 96 in a Test at the SCG against the West Indies in 1989. From then on captains assumed they could chuck the ball at anyone who could bowl slowly and he would do the business. So imagine how I felt turning up for my second Test start there in 1991. We even played two spinners — I was partnered by Eddie Hemmings in a cricketing version of the Little and Large Show.

But the Tufnell nerve held outwardly at least and I managed to get a five-for in their second dig. I would have had a hat-trick as well but David Gower could not hang on to a stinging chance from Dean Jones.

Is For...
Tabloids
Tail
Terror Track
Third Umpire
Thorpey
Tits & Arse
Touring
Trescothick
Twenty20 Cricket

Tabloids

As the subject of the odd tabloid headline on front and back pages, I nearly pissed myself when I heard the one about the reporter who was caught bang to rights in his own paper's honeytrap. Apparently, on one England tour, a red top Fleet Street title had paid a couple of high-class hookers to hang around the lobby of our hotel and see if they could entice one of the boys into some extra-curricular physical jerks.

Perfect stuff for the paper. Set the bait and sit back and wait while some half-cut cricketer, who hasn't had a shag for a couple of weeks, falls for it hook, line and sinker. All over the front and back pages "cricket ace scores with hooker" or "England star bowls maiden over" — the normal sort of tosh. So they were a bit upset when they heard that one of their employees — one of Fleet Street's finest and most distinguished scribblers — along with a former player, had been lining up the girls for themselves in the foyer.

Cue frantic calls from news desk to cricket correspondent to tell him that that particular piece of crumpet was off limits. And, yes, they would be looking closely at his expenses next time he was in the office. Very sweet.

The stunts that some of the tabs pull do the England team more harm than good. Take the time that Mark Taylor brought his Aussie team over for the Ashes in 1997 and was facing the chop because he couldn't get a run.

One of the rags thought it would be a good idea to go and buttonhole Tubs and present him with a bat that was about four feet wide. Result at Edgbaston in the first Test: Taylor c and b Croft 129. Although England won the game it might have been a bit easier without Taylor's first hundred for two years, which saw him hang onto the captaincy and ultimately the Ashes. It makes you wonder whose side they are on sometimes.

Tail

The tail in a cricket team can stretch all the way from number 10 to number 11, or less if you are Australian, but mostly it goes from about number eight down to the last man in. (English tails have been known to start at number six). If the last few boys get the scoreboard ticking over then the tail is said to have "wagged." Not when I've been involved it hasn't.

In 1999 England played New Zealand at The Oval and boasted a tail comprising of Ed Giddins, Phil Tufnell and Alan Mullally. I'll hold my hands up and admit we were hardly in the Bradman class but some of the papers had written us off before we started. They were saying that England had only picked eight players who could hold a bat and in effect had picked three number elevens.

That's almost slanderous. I'll have you know that all three of us managed to keep our bats in our hands while we were at the wicket. I am also proud to announce that I batted number ten in both innings and relegated the new-boy Giddins to the bottom of the pile.

I am doubly proud to announce that in the first dig our three-man 'tail' detained the Kiwi bowling for more than three-quarters of an hour and added 12 runs while second time round we were slightly less prolific, piling up a mighty five runs.

Seriously, the days of having three rabbits at the bottom of the order seem to have gone, and every player at Test level is expected to contribute something to the runs column. Although you still don't expect to see a specialist batsman turning his arm over unless you are trying to get the opposition to declare.

There is nothing so frustrating as reducing a side to 200 for five and seeing the last five wickets double the score. The Australians and the South Africans have proved to be the masters at this over the last couple of years.

Terror Track

I used to class any pitch on which the ball got above ankle height as a terror track.

Third Umpire

The arrival of the third umpire, armed with his half dozen cameras, proved once and for all that cricket has always been a batsman's game.

As a result of cameras being used to judge close run outs we have seen that nine times out of ten a direct hit is out. Therefore there are a lot of lucky former batsmen around whose average is much higher than it might have been because they were never given out when they were run out in the dim and distant past.

Overall the use of the video ref for line decisions has worked out well and has sharpened up some of the running between the wickets — you don't see that many batsmen coasting into the crease now but it should stop there.

As I have said elsewhere umpires can set the tone of the day's play and I don't want to see them relegated to hat-stands. "Give us your sweater, I'll count to six, and we'll turn round" sort of thing.

As usual these things depend on television because most third umpires are using the TV feed to make the decision — no good if the cameras are not in line with the stumps as happened once in Australia. I didn't make that trip (Stewie was captain) but England lost the last Test at Sydney, to go down 3-1 instead of drawing 2-2, because the cameras were not in the right place.

Michael Slater was on 35 when a direct hit from Dean Headley saw him run out. Until it was referred upstairs and the ump in the box, Simon Taufel, found out that as the cameras were not exactly in line with the stumps he couldn't see clearly because Peter Such had got in the way. Back in Tufnell Towers I was choking on my nightcap.

Slater had his gloves off and was ready to go back to the pavilion until the third umpire was called on. He made 123 and England lost a series they possibly could have squared.

Using the video for catches, though, has got out of hand. Now a batsman can dolly one up in the air just in front of mid-off and stand his ground knowing that if it goes to the cameras there is a decent chance he will be given not out. Dermot Reeve demonstrated it for all to see on television when he showed up the limitations of camera shots which try to demonstrate whether the ball has carried or not. Most players know if they have caught the ball and it is cobblers to say they don't.

They are trying to make a two-dimensional decision in a three-dimensional situation and it just doesn't work so let's just leave it at the line decisions.

Thorpey

Thorpey was the third and final member of the 'bat pack' to make his Test debut, and unlike Ramps and Nasser, he made an immediate impact by taking a ton off the Aussies and making instant headlines.

He was a fixture from then on and, although he got criticised for not converting enough half-centuries into three figures, he always batted for the team and not for himself. He would come in and blaze to a quick 60 or 70, as he did three times against South Africa in 1994, and suddenly we would have the momentum with us and the upper hand in the match.

Those innings were far more valuable than a long hundred that might have looked better in the book and in someone's career batting figures.

He was the main man in the England batting line-up for a long time in the nineties and would have got into most sides in the world. But for such a good player sometimes he managed to look as if he couldn't give a toss.

That probably says more about my skills in reading people than it does about Thorpey, but I just thought sometimes that he had the air of someone who would rather have been somewhere else.

At the end of one Test series we were all jumping about at The Oval looking forward to a trip to South Africa with all the chaps on board when Thorpey piped up that actually he wasn't going on tour. We didn't have a clue that he was thinking about staying behind but it didn't seem like it was that big a deal for him not to be going.

To be honest, after what he went through, he probably did want to be somewhere other than a sweaty dressing room full of leery cricketers and I can understand that point of view.

For someone who had plenty of problems of his own he was a great listener to other people's woes. He was a big support to me when I was going slightly nuts in Australia and spent hours hearing me pouring out my heart which probably pushed him close to the edge, although if it did he didn't show it.

Despite all that he was consistently England's leading batsman and I know the Aussies valued his wicket higher than anyone else's. Now he seems to have moved on from his domestic troubles he could be in the England side for a few years yet.

In his own quiet way he was a bit of a rebel as well and we got on well. He didn't like being told what to do and if we had to wear shoes of a certain colour to an official do you could bet your bottom Benson that Thorpey would turn up in a completely different colour.

Tits & Arse

Cocktail parties were not really my thing when I was a kid on tour with England — I usually had to be dragged kicking and screaming by my official MCC tour tie to these functions. I used to think they were about as exciting as watching paint dry. I would grab a handful of canapes, a quick livener and I was out of the door, making my excuses before going out on the tiles. But once I had stayed at one for longer than 10 minutes I realised what a giggle could be had with a bit of imagination.

Think about it. Tray upon tray of free fizz, food, lots of mature rich crumpet and 16 finely tuned young male athletes on the prowl and miles from home — the perfect setting for a game of 'T and A,' I first played 'Tits and Arse' in India in 1993 and pretty quickly discovered that I had a definite aptitude for the game. The object as the name suggests, is to grope as many breasts and buttocks (female) as possible in a designated period of time, usually an hour, which is as long as it took for me to get past my career batting average.

Let's face, it these women have been stuck out in colonies for half their life and welcome a spot of harmless flirting so it's not hard to rack up a quick fifty (Two points T, one point A, bonus of five for the ambassador's wife). A peck on the cheek when you are introduced to your prey, hand slips round the rear for a cheeky single before coming back for the two-pointer on the way up. A flustered look, and your street cred with your watching team-mates is now through the roof. All good clean fun.

Touring

Being an England cricketer on tour sounds like a fantastic job, and mostly it is, but it is not all beer and skittles. On my many England trips I have been admitted to hospital, had golf balls hit at me from a particularly unfriendly crowd, been accused of smoking pot in a restaurant and been fined for kicking my cap when our keeper dropped a catch off me. (I wouldn't have minded paying the money, but it was Sachin Tendulkar). Cricket is the only sport which asks players to be away from home for more than three months at a time and that can have repercussions back home for some players.

Still, going with England does have its compensations. I don't know how it works but the old England training top is a bit of a magnet for crumpet and generally you don't go short of the company of top quality young females.

When you get picked for a tour all you have to remember to take to the airport is your toothbrush, a passport and your best bowling boots. The batsman always have a bit more clobber than the bowlers but by cutting down on my kit I could get more duty-free in my case.

Once you get out to the Caribbean, Australia or wherever, you are treated like a king by most of the locals and on the subcontinent the attention you get is almost suffocating.

Everything on tour is done for you. If you want to sit in your hotel and live on room service you can. If you fancy a game of golf on your day off then it is fixed up and if friends need tickets for the games they can usually be rustled up.

You can get used to having people running around after you and I've had my eyes opened since I retired. I've got a little sideline business that organises tours for sports fans, England in the Windies, where people can visit my old haunts, and rugby trips abroad.

Being Phil Tufnell tour leader is a bit different from being Phil Tufnell touring England cricketer. Nowadays I have to try and organise other people's lives for them instead of having my arse wiped. With a reputation like mine? It would have been unthinkable a couple of years ago. Phil Tufnell, the bad tourist, now taking parties of people abroad? What would Ray lllingworth have to say about that?

We took some people to Dublin for the England rugby team's Grand Slam match against the Irish and I'm afraid to say all my old touring instincts took over. After about three hours kip in three days I looked a bit crumpled. How did I manage to keep it up on a three-month trip and play cricket in between as well?

Trescothick

Marcus Trescothick, or Banger to his mates, was one of Duncan Fletcher's selectorial picks that really came off, and he can give the ball a fearful thump when he is in the mood.

I remember hearing about this kid who made 300 in a second team match, had captained the age-group England sides and who was going to be a superstar. He was obviously groomed for it but we didn't hear from him for a few years.

Duncan Fletcher obviously rated him though and had no hesitation in putting him in the side even when his county record was a bit thin. He was proved right with knobs on.

Then came the inevitable slide. It is no disgrace to have a bad trot against Australia but as soon as you do have a bad trot people start analysing your technique.

With Banger, when he was on song, he never moved his feet much and when he was not on song he never moved his feet. Obviously if he's not scoring runs people will blame the fact that he doesn't move his feet, but he was hardly Fred Astaire when he worked his way into the England side was he?

The worst thing that can happen is for people to meddle with his technique. He's big enough and ugly enough to sort out his own game, and I'm sure he will.

Twenty20 Cricket

I must admit I smiled to myself when it was announced that

the final of the Twenty20 Cup was going to be played at Trent Bridge and not at Lord's.

This quickfire game is probably not appreciated at HQ anyway, people look like they are enjoying themselves too much, but the real reason they had to move was because they couldn't get an entertainment licence for the ground. And rather than give Atomic Kitten the elbow they moved the final to Nottingham.

I would have loved to have seen the Scouse girl-band playing at Lord's — especially 'Rear of the Year' Natasha Hamilton. The look on the faces of the chaps in front of the pavilion would have been worth the admission money alone.

Is For...
Umpires
Uncovered Pitches
Underarm
Universities
Up The Other End

Umpires

Ever since meeting the real men in white coats in a Perth psychiatric unit I have tried to give the ones on the pitch a wide berth because they can do some serious damage to your figures if you get on the wrong side of them.

It is best not to appeal too much because some umps are less likely to give you a decision if you have been in his earhole the whole day, but you've got to get the balance right because if you don't ask now and then you'll get nothing.

Some officials are more sympathetic to bowlers than others, however, and if I knew one (who was well known on the circuit as being on the bowler's side) was standing in one of our games I'd be grabbing the ball off the skipper before 11.30.

Being an 'outer' has nothing to do with exposing celebrity homosexuals but more to do with pointing batsmen in the direction of the pavilion when the ball's pitched just outside leg stump. There are a few 'outers' on the county treadmill (no names, no pack-drill lads — just keep on sticking that finger up and you'll get my vote) but they are completely outnumbered by 'not outers.'

So it makes sense for a bowler to keep on the right side of the umps and not wind them up the wrong way. As soon as any umpire thinks you are being a smart arse you can kiss goodbye to your five-for and that touch-and-go LBW.

A good umpire should control the atmosphere of the game without interfering with the match itself — something most of the old boys on the Test and county circuit manage to do.

But some of the blokes who officiate on tour seem to think they are in showbiz and have to get noticed to get a Test match gig. There are guys you run into when you play tour games down under who think they are conducting an orchestra when they are signalling a boundary. I'm all for some of the theatricals and jazzing the game up a bit but you've got to make sure you get the decisions right as well.

I'm afraid my temper snapped with one of these so-called characters when we were playing in New Zealand. I had just seen my bowling launched for yet another six when this clown started signalling the score as if he was conducting the

London Symphony Orchestra. There are not many similarities between PCR Tufnell and WG Grace, but I regret to inform you I borrowed one of the bearded one's one-liners then. Something along the lines of, "They haven't come here to see you umpire, they've come to see us play cricket." Looking back, it was probably not the smartest thing to say when my bowling was disappearing all over the park.

There were a few characters umpiring on the county circuit when I was a player and I couldn't believe the lengths some of them went to to do the job. I mean they're hardly going to finish up as millionaires are they? If we thought we stayed in some pretty dingy B&Bs it was nothing compared to what some of the umpires put themselves through. Alan Whitehead used to travel everywhere in a caravan and they all usually had to have other jobs to keep some sort of cash coming in. David Shepherd, one of the world's top white coaters, used to have a post office in Devon.

Although I had the odd run-in with the officials I doff my reversed baseball hat in their direction for their contribution to the game.

Uncovered Pitches

Uncovered pitches are another topic that get the 'In my day' brigade straight out of their bath-chairs and to be honest I have sympathy with them on this one.

Nowadays the boys wheel the covers out as soon as there is a black spot in the sky and the uniform nature of the surfaces that we play cricket on nowadays does nothing for players' techniques. Batsmen would have to learn to vary the way they play according to the surface and the spinners would get the occasional 'sticky dog' to have a bowl on.

Derek Underwood, a fellow slow left-armer, made a living out of bowling sides out on a 'sticky dog' — a wicket that has had a bit of rain on it. He was absolutely lethal on a pitch that had a bit of water on it (although he was a decent bowler when the pitch was covered as well) and I wouldn't have minded having a pot at bowling on a rain-affected surface. I had better get back into that bath-chair and have a sit down.

Underarm

You can't bowl underarm nowadays which is a shame because it would be quite comical to see one of the quicks sprint into the crease before sinking into the old Crown Green position and rolling a pea-shooter down to the other end of the pitch. Adam Gilchrist could probably still get enough height on it to clear the boundary though.

Trevor Chappell delivered an infamous underarm delivery for Australia against New Zealand in 1981. It was bound to happen sometime but it had to involve the Chappells (Greg was captain) didn't it? The Kiwis needed six off the last ball to tie the one-dayer in Melbourne so Greg told his little brother to bowl underarm.

Of course everyone went potty and the underarm delivery was outlawed. I know it's easy to say after the event but you didn't have to be a fortune-teller to see it was going to happen one day.

Universities

Playing cricket against the universities used to be a jolly way to start off the season, but there is no way the games should have been included in your figures.

Think about it from my point of view. I would not hit peak fitness until, at least, July, once I had shrugged off the excesses of the winter, and the last thing you are going to get at The Parks in April is a track with something in it for the twirlers.

I would also take advantage of the liberal hospitality bestowed on us by the students only to pay the price the next day. When you are supposed to be an England bowler and you are doing your best to impress the bit of posh totty in the spotty dress on the boundary you need things to go your way. What you definitely do not need is a seamer's track, a raging hangover and a rugby player at the other end with the eye of Viv Richards who is intent on finding favour with the same bit of skirt you've got your eye on.

So later in my career I always tried to give the student games a body swerve. It is no good going down there with your England sweater on giving it the big 'un and getting tonked.

Up The Other End

Whoever said the best place to face fast bowling, and it was probably a batsman with his average on his mind, was from up the other end almost gets my vote. The best place to play the really quick stuff is from your unsponsored motor in the car park. Then there is absolutely no danger, as Tubs Taylor used to say, of "having to wear a couple."

Is For...
Vaughan
Venus
Viv

Vaughan

When Michael Vaughan pitched up at the wicket in Johannesburg with England two for two, on what they used to call a sporting pitch and with Alan Donald bowling like lightning he must have thought the world had gone mad. Pretty soon afterwards we were two for four and Vaughany hadn't faced a single ball. Not much in county cricket prepares you for that but within four years he was the best batsman in the world according to the number crunchers.

In that first Test against the Boks he nudged it around for 30-odd but there was no real sign he would turn into a world-class player. So imagine my surprise when I turned on the box in the middle of the night, during the last Ashes tour, and there was Virgil giving Glenn McGrath and Shane Warne the long handle. I rubbed my eyes again and still the Yorkie was dishing out the stick to two of the best bowlers who have ever turned their arm over.

Then I read the papers, it really had happened and it hadn't been a dream. An English batsman socking it to the Aussies on their own patch and batting like Adam Gilchrist in a blue helmet. Happy days.

People asked why it had taken so long for England to discover him but the truth is he only discovered himself when he was about 27 years old. All of a sudden he got that extra bit of confidence to take the bowlers on and bingo he was the top-rated bat in the world.

I always fancied my chances of getting him out when we played the Yorkies in the County Championship but he has gone up to another level now and to be frank I'm probably better off wrestling snakes than bowling at him. Let's just keep our fingers crossed that he stays fit and we can pencil him into the England line-up for the next ten years.

He has always had a good technique and when he started to play more aggressively he looked on another planet to the rest of the England line-up. All we need now is another six Vaughans.

Venus

As soon as the words "Venus being in the wrong juxtaposition with somewhere else" had tripped out of Lord Ted Dexter's mouth in 1993, the sage of North London must have known he was for the high jump.

Coming off the back of England's seventh successive defeat did not help his cause and the media duly laid into his rantings. The only reason that the defeat at Lord's was our seventh on the spin was that we had been playing as if we had just stepped off a spaceship and never seen a cricket ball in our lives.

The press made the most of this unexpected soundbite and Lord Ted was crucified before eventually resigning towards the end of the summer. The remark was typical of him. For someone who I thought would be completely old school tie he was totally unconventional with his motorbike and leather jackets. I just don't think his man-management was of the highest class. He was literally on another planet.

Ironically the last team he was involved with picking was the one which beat Australia (admittedly in a dead Test) at The Oval at the end of 1993. Although I was back in the squad after a couple of games off I didn't make the cut but the big man Fraser started after two-and-a-half years out of the team with his hip injury.

Gus ended up with eight wickets in the match and a legend was reborn, so Dexter the stargazer got one thing right at least. He put his foot in it good and proper with Ian Botham once, though. Beefy had been tapped up about going to South Africa on an unofficial tour in 1989-90 and had been offered a three-year deal by Ali Bacher.

But Beefy wanted to have one more crack at the West Indies and told all and sundry he was available to tour the Caribbean — only for Dexter to ring him and say he wasn't being picked for the trip after all. Beefy's reply is not recorded but I would have fancied earwigging that phone call.

Viv

Getting Viv Richards out at The Oval in 1991 was one of the highlights of my career. I had watched in awe for years as he battered bowlers around without wearing a helmet. So to get him in my back pocket early on takes some beating.

It was quite simple really and I don't know why bowlers didn't cotton on to how to bowl to the Master Blaster about 20 years earlier. On second thoughts I witnessed some of the carnage so let's just say I was a bit lucky and Viv smashed one up in the air when he was trying to hit me somewhere in the direction of Croydon.

If you think that footballers are worshipped in England you should go to Antigua and check out the telephone directory. Even David Beckham wouldn't appear on the front of the yellow pages in England. Viv does in Antigua.

Is For...
Wagon Wheel
Walking
Warne
Waughs
Wellington
Western Terrace
Willow
World Championship
World Cups

Wagon Wheel

I always thought that Wagon Wheels were the chocolate biscuits I shoved down my neck when I went to Highbury to watch the Arse but apparently batsmen have them as well.

They are little charts that show where each shot went in their innings and those for someone like Sachin Tendulkar have shots all round the wicket, making a very satisfying pattern.

Mine leave something to be desired usually having only one trail from the wicket to somewhere in the vicinity of first slip or the keeper. There are not many of them hanging up on the walls at Lord's.

Walking

The old saying that Aussies only walk when their cars break down was kicked into touch when Adam Gilchrist gave himself out in the 2003 World Cup. Gilly trooped off the pitch after feathering one to the Sri Lanka keeper in the semi-final and walked straight into the sort of reception normally received for someone who has just cured world poverty.

Now I am all for batsmen walking when they have nicked one because the poor old bowler has enough trouble getting them out once let alone twice. Brian Lara is a batsman who tends to walk, imagine his figures if he didn't.

But I am afraid Gilly, that if you have turned into Mother Theresa then you've got to bin all the appeals for non-existent edges and for stumpings when you know the batsman is a yard in. It works both ways, chaps.

Warne

You've got to hand it to Warnie. The world's best spinner said he wanted to go out of his last World Cup with a bang and I think we can safely say he managed that.

The anti-drugs boys wanted to land a big fish and although he has slimmed down a bit they don't come any bigger than SK Warne, so the authorities managed to hook up the cricketing equivalent of Moby Dick and Jaws rolled into one.

When his first urine sample came back positive for a

diuretic, I thought the Aussie physio would be for the high jump because everything you put in your mouth nowadays has to pass the medical team, but then Warnie said it was his mum. Poor old Bridgette Warne suddenly became the most notorious mother in the sport since Mrs Chappell's offspring started bowling underarm at New Zealanders.

He claimed he had used the drugs once before to get rid of a bloated chin when he had consumed one too many bottles of his new wine Chateau Googly. I'm sorry mate, but when I've had a skinful of Shiraz the last thing I'm worried about is my double chin, which may or may not be shifted by popping a pill. Still, after all these years taking the piss out of batsmen, it was a bit ironic that some of Warnie's urine should put him in front of the beak.

He obviously rushed back too quickly from the shoulder injury he got in the VB Series, but he was gambling with the rest of his cricketing career and, as I said at the time, he should have stuck to the less incriminating beer and fags like the rest of us.

The year's ban might have been two, and that could have been that for the tubby turner, but at least he kept the old twirlymen in the news. And he earned me a few quid as well. As soon as the news came out that Warnie was on his way back to Oz without even turning his dodgy shoulder the Tufnell mobile was red-hot with calls from journalists and radio stations wanting some reaction. And I was only too happy to oblige. Cheers Warnie.

There are not many cricketers around who can get the sport onto the front pages of the broadsheets, although I've managed a few red-top headlines in the past, but Warne is one of them. He has been making the news ever since he burst onto the cricket scene looking like a blonde beach ball from Bondi. He was the biggest spinner ever seen until the Labour party got their bullshit merchants working.

His 'Ball of the Century' in 1993 turned the width of two Mike Gattings leaving Gatt, a superb player of spin, looking like someone who had never seen a ball veer off the straight and the Aussie fielders speechless. Which takes some doing.

He made slow bowling trendy again and it was no surprise

when he was voted one of the Five Cricketers of the Century by *Wisden*. But some of the scrapes he has got into, even before his luminous piss sample came back from the lab, make me proud to be a member of the spinners' union.

He lost his chance at the full-time Australian captaincy after admitting to telephone sex with a 22-year-old nurse who he met in a Leicester nightclub when he was playing at Hampshire.

Now the county circuit can be a lonely place and cricketers can be vulnerable to the advances of the opposite sex but fancy blowing a job like that and not even getting a shag. He would have been a great skipper as well. He showed in a few games in charge of the one-day team that he was prepared to take a gamble and in common with most spinners he was a big thinker about the game.

If he fell down a public bog though he would come up with a Mars bar in his mouth. Even when he admitted taking money from a bookie, the mysterious John, he came up smelling of roses because the Aussie board kept it under wraps, so they copped all the criticism.

In Antigua in 1999 he was caught by a snapper with a fag in his hand after being paid $200,000 to give up the weed and the same happened in New Zealand a couple of years later. Although the thought of bowling at Brian Lara at St John's and the effects of the local rum can be used as an excuse for not packing in the gaspers and sneaking off for a quick puff.

He has come through all these scrapes virtually unscathed and that is down to one thing. He is a genius with a ball in his hands and most sports fans give people like Warnie a bit of leeway. That's why people in England still love George Best. Because of Warnie's impact, kids all over the world have started bowling leggies and flippers and most Test sides have a decent exponent of wrist spin (although the search, like the one for the Next Botham, goes on in England). But unlike Best, Warne has fulfilled all of his potential on the pitch and in terms of projecting cricket to the masses is the most exhilirating thing to happen to the game since Beefy started smashing it about.

It was while Warne was captaining Oz in a day-nighter against England in Melbourne in 1999 that he saved our lads from getting decapitated. The Aussie fans had obviously been on the old VB all evening and decided to test the England boys' reflexes by lobbing a few well-aimed golf and snooker balls at the fielders.

Stewie was England captain at the time and asked Warnie to calm down his home crowd. The local hero did this by nicking Mark Waugh's helmet and putting it on as he walked towards the mob. They stopped chucking stuff and the game was back on.

Pretty soon afterwards Australia coasted to the win that Warnie had masterminded. No wonder they love him.

Waughs

There is a sign in the home dressing room at the Sydney Cricket Ground that just about sums up Steve Waugh. It is a quote from Waugh himself, which is framed and hung above the door the Aussie batsmen walk through before they start thrashing touring bowlers to all parts of the old ground.

It says "The big occasion is the one you have been waiting for — the chance to do something great." Steve Waugh saves himself for the big occasion and the tougher the opposition the more he performs. His twin Mark is not a bad player either.

In fact, when Ian Chappell was asked once, before Mark had made his Test debut, if Steve Waugh was the best allrounder in the world he replied that he wasn't even the best allrounder in his family.

In 1995 when the Australians, led by Mark Taylor, won a series in the Caribbean for the first time in more than 20 years, only two of the tourists' batsmen managed more than 200 runs in the four match series. No surprises for guessing that Steve Waugh was top with 429 and Mark Waugh second in the list with 240. None of Taylor, David Boon, Michael Slater, Greg Blewett or Ian Healey made more than 160 in the whole series.

The twins set up a win in the deciding Test in Jamaica with a stand of 231 that broke the Windies and even had Winston Benjamin crying like a baby during one drinks interval. Steve helped himself to a double ton even though he was disturbed in the middle of the night by a burglar. But he had showed the

West Indians he meant business in the Test in Trinidad that the Aussies lost.

With Curtly Ambrose steaming in on a greentop, Steve played and missed nearly every other ball until big Curts couldn't take it any longer and went mad. He ran down the pitch and had to be pulled back by Richie Richardson as he cursed the Australian. I swear Curtly was ready to deck him.

Waugh just stood there like John Wayne in a Wild West film and stared back at him with those narrow eyes before unleashing a few expletives of his own. Talk about bollocks. He ended up 60-odd not out from 128, and, sure, the Aussies lost but he had made his point.

That was vintage Waugh, just as his hundred at the SCG against England on the last Ashes tour was. Then he was under the cosh from the word go and even the Aussies were saying he was too old and should step aside. So it was only natural he would go out and get a ton, passing 10,000 Test runs and equalling the Don's record of 29 Test hundreds.

Great players don't give others the chance to shape their careers and it would have been easy for the Aussie selectors to draw a line under the Waugh era after the Ashes. But 'The Iceman' kept piling up the runs and made it impossible for him to be left out of the tour of the Caribbean. Waugh reckoned he had unfinished business in the West Indies and in India.

Of the two brothers, Steve played the percentages while Mark was the gambler who always gave you a chance to get him out. But it wasn't always like that. Steve started as a bit of a dasher but reined himself in — cutting out the hook almost completely — later on in his career. Mark was a great player to watch as long as you didn't have to bowl at him. If you were bowling and he had a good hour your figures were usually beyond repair.

I had the misfortune to play against Mark on his Test debut in Adelaide on the 1990-1 tour down under. The sensitive Australians dropped Steve after 42 Tests for his younger twin brother who promptly scored one of the best hundreds I've ever seen. Apparently when Mark told Steve he'd been picked, Steve asked him which "mug have they dropped"? To which Mark could only say "er... you, mate."

That day I just couldn't bowl at Mark and he cut me to death to romp to 138 and although I got him a few times later in my career (see Bunny) I couldn't get a sniff then. No-one could call him Afghanistan (The Forgotten War) after that knock.

The pair of them served notice of their talents when they put on 464 for New South Wales against Western Australia in Perth. There was a third Waugh brother Dean, who played a couple of first-class games, who would undoubtedly have been christened the Third World Waugh — but thankfully for bowlers everywhere he has not played Test cricket.

Wellington

I didn't have that much success at the Basin Reserve in Wellington, but that's not the reason I have such bad memories of the place. In 1992 Beefy played his 100th Test there, but the match is remembered more for the awful injury that David 'Syd' Lawrence suffered and which threatened to turn the match into a mass brawl.

Syd was a big old unit and his action was always going to put a huge stress on his knees, Fred Astaire he was not.

When he went down clutching his knee as he came into bowl we all knew something was badly wrong. He was put on a stretcher and as Beefy and a couple of the boys carried him off a cameraman pointed the lens of his camera right into Syd's face.

Beefy, of course, went bananas and threatened to stick the offending piece of equipment where the sun don't shine and after a minor scuffle he was led away.

But I couldn't believe that someone would do that when a bloke had clearly suffered a career-threatening injury.

Another thing I remember about that game is that I had to bowl 71 overs in the first innings. My reward was two for a lot and a pair of feet that looked like they had been attacked by a cheese grater. It's not all glamour this international cricket lark.

Western Terrace

I could never work out what all the fuss was about when people complained about the Western Terrace. The racist chants were out of order and obviously there is no place for that anywhere, let alone at cricket grounds, but most of the punters in the old stand at Headingley were just lads on a day out.

On the very rare occasions when I played there (England don't go for spinners up in Leeds) the crowd in the "notorious Western Terrace" as the liberal papers put it, seemed to take to me, probably because my reputation was more grey than whiter-than-white. Of course, Goughie is their hero because they can all relate to someone like the Dazzler, and he plays up to them in return.

The fans there love to dress up and it has caught on at several of the Test grounds in England, obviously not in St John's Wood though, where spectators will turn up to the match dressed as a piece of fruit, Elvis Presley or the Teletubbies. A teacher was once kicked out for turning up dressed as a carrot. Some of the crusty colonel types object to it but cricket needs all the dosh it can get and if someone is prepared to pay fifty quid to come to the cricket and get plastered while dressed up as Fred Flintstone then we can't afford to turn them away.

Willow

Don't ever share a room on tour with a batsman. They are obsessed with their bats, which usually have names like Hercules or Excalibur, and would rather spend all night in their room talking to lumps of willow than chatting up some of the local talent.

Nasser and Thorpey are the worst of the lot. The pair of them would sit up all night altering their bats by shaving bits off the bottom, adding some metal tape to them or putting on rubber grips. So, instead of doing their bit for the image of the Englishman abroad and sinking a few coldies, when we were on foreign trips they wasted all their spare time tinkering with bits of wood in the hope that their average would improve by a decimal point or two.

If you are rooming with a willow merchant then make sure you get into the room first. If the batsman gets first run then by the time you arrive your bed will be covered with a line of bats ready to be sandpapered. The bedroom will be full of tape, scissors, pads, thigh pads, boxes and gloves and your room-mate will be talking to them as he gives them the once over with chamois leather. And it will all be obsessively lined-up and tidy. If a psychiatrist walked into the room the occupants would be locked up and have the key thrown away.

Athers was the exception among the willow merchants. He couldn't have given a toss about the state of his room and just threw his batting stuff into the corner before settling down with a book full of long words. But when he was captain he had his own room anyway. (From 1996 we all got our own rooms).

Bowlers by contrast are a dream to share with. All a bowler needs is a pair of boots and once he knows his boots are safe he is ready to go out on the town.

Usually, when you check-in to a new hotel on tour, you arrange to meet in the bar before hitting the town. The entire bowling attack will be knocking back sherbets within five minutes of dumping their kit but those higher up the order will not be seen for at least three hours while they make sure their bats have settled into their new room. How sad is that?

World Championship

It was a brave decision by the boffins to try and work out a way of deciding who really was the best Test side in the world. Even if it is completely obvious, as it is at the moment.

We can't have a proper World Cup of Test cricket because that would take even longer than the last one-day World Cup and would have to be held all over the world like a travelling circus so that no-one could complain that the conditions were unfair.

No matter how good the system the ICC put in place, however, it was always going to make a rick at some point and when South Africa were handed the trophy for being the world's best Test side I had to suppress a chuckle.

Australia are comfortably the best side in the world and probably will be for the next decade but they lost the title because one of their tours got cancelled, and South Africa managed to hammer Bangladesh. People took the piss out of the ICC but trying to work out who the World Champions of

Tests are, when the teams are on a bit more of a level playing field, will take someone with the brains of Brearley.

World Cups

When you cross the old white line for England in any form of cricket it gives you a massive buzz, but there is something special about a World Cup. I'm not having a dig at the Test game because that is the best and most satisfying form of cricket to play, but for sense of occasion the World Cup takes some beating.

The whole of the host country is concentrating on cricket for once and all the top boys from around the world are in the same place at the same time.

I was hardly renowned as a one-day specialist but I did manage to tip up to one World Cup as a player in Australia and New Zealand in 1992 and it was one of the highlights of my career.

You could wander through your hotel lobby and bump into Kapil Dev, Malcolm Marshall or Imran Khan shooting the breeze and for a young kid like me it was a bit nerve-wracking just to rub shoulders with giants of the game like these blokes. The cricket was a bit of an eye-opener too.

Each World Cup brings a new tactic. In 1996 it was pinch-hitting, when the openers — led by the Sri Lankans — went out all guns blazing from the word go to take advantage of the 15-over fielding restrictions and the scoreboard rattled along like a machine gun.

In 1992 the New Zealanders played the Aussies in the first game of the tournament and opened the bowling with their off-spinner old Dipak Patel. The Kiwis won and Martin Crowe their captain was hailed as a tactical genius in the Mike Brearley mould.

Sitting in the team hotel watching old Sixpack turning his arm in the second over of the innings got me thinking back to my old days as a new ball bowler at school. Steaming in off a long run and knocking batsmen's heads off was the order of the day then but this was different.

Taking the pace of the ball and using an orthodox spinner to do it was just common sense and the extra bounce the new ball gets comes in just as handy for a spinner as it does for one of the speed merchants.

To say I was getting excited when I was named in the team for England's first match against India would be a bit wide of the mark. I was crapping myself at the thought of being given first crack with a shiny new conker in international cricket. Surely we would be just as adventurous as the New Zealanders and open with a twirlyman?

Me, Phil Tufnell, England's new ball bowler? With my reputation?

Sadly Graham Gooch, who was our skipper in the tournament, did not see eye to eye tactically with the Kiwis or else he must have had some reservations about entrusting the new ball to the argumentative ragamuffin spinner who had tormented him the previous winter.

After that tournament it became old-hat for spinners to open the bowling and my chance of forging a legendary new ball partnership with Daffy DeFreitas or Chris Lewis had gone. Imagine a Tufnell- Gough opening pair, that would have threatened Trueman and Statham if we had had the chance. In my dreams, anyway.

The following World Cup was held in the subcontinent and I watched it from afar as England went from one cock-up to another. Athers wrote a detailed report to the English authorities after the tournament and they managed to ignore most of his recommendations. The next two have followed the same pattern as far as England are concerned.

I went to the last World Cup with a different brief. I was in with the media lads (or the Beastie Boys as they used to be known) and saw it from another angle, sometimes horizontal after I had got stuck into the hospitality.

On a serious note, the tournament was well organised even if the crowds dipped when South Africa were knocked out but it was way too long. In the first World Cup in 1975 there were 15 matches and in 1987 in India and Pakistan there were 27.

The World Cup in South Africa featured more than 50 games which is at least 15 too many. By the time the Super Sixes started most of the fans and media could hardly remember

Brian Lara's fantastic hundred in the opening game that put the skids under the hosts.

For the next World Cup, if I am appointed commissioner, which with my experience of touring in the Caribbean should be a certainty, I would reduce the number of games. Keep in the minnows, by all means, but there should not be more than one per group.

Having four groups of four with the top two going through to the straight knock-out quarter-finals would reduce the number of games and keep the interest in the tournament going without staleness creeping in for players and fans.

And what a shindig the next World Cup promises to be. The people in the Caribbean are potty about cricket and if the Windies have a glimmer of a chance the place will be absolutely jumping. It might be worth giving a couple of games to the Americans despite the obvious Mickey Mouse jibes that it would attract.

No-one's asking for them to take up the game permanently but there are enough Asians and West Indians in parts of America to make it worthwhile for a one-off. The football World Cup when it was held there attracted full houses even if the men's game did not catch on. There is half a chance I might make an appearance.

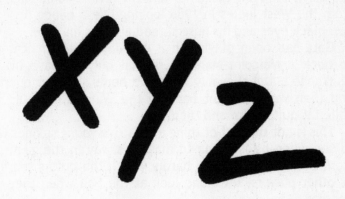

Is For...
X-rated
X-rays
Yips
Yorker
Zimbabwe
Zone
Zooter

X-rated

When I was starting out at Middlesex I was made well aware of the perils of facing quick bowlers when Gatt came back early from the West Indies in 1986 looking like a panda bear with two black eyes and his nose spread all over his face.

Gatt had been playing in a one-dayer in Jamaica, tried to hook a Malcolm Marshall special only to have his face rearranged. Unbelievably he came home, had an operation and then went straight back to the Windies. I would have called it quits there and then.

This is not the sort of thing a sensitive young spinner wants to see when he is trying to make his way in the game, and from that day on I could hardly watch the quicks tearing in at other players, let alone look at the ball when they were heading in my direction.

X-rays

I've been lucky, or clever, enough not to make too many visits to the x-ray department but Lord's did use x-rays to pull the wool over the eyes of the Aussies when they wanted to take the Ashes back down under.

The men at Lord's had the urn x-rayed and lo and behold they found a fracture. So they said, "Sorry lads. The Ashes are staying here at the museum even though we haven't won them for nearly 20 years we're keeping them."

Better still, the crack is more than 75 years old and the MCC said there was degeneration of the adhesive that was part of the original repair. Sounds like get stuffed fellas to you and me.

Yips

Golfers are famous for getting the yips — a sort of uncontrollable nervous shudder under pressure — and some like Bernhard Langer have had them two or three times and recovered. But it's easy for them. They can take three, four or five putts then go to the practice green and iron out the problem. When a bowler gets the yips he's got to finish the over and there's a bloke at the other end with a bat trying to hit the ball that bounces three times out of the ground.

For bowlers, the yips can come in several forms; from the inability to hit the cut stuff to not even being able to let go of the ball. Phil Edmonds even forgot how many steps he had in his run-up on a tour in India (it was four) and was reduced to bowling off one pace. He bowled brilliantly, taking 32 wickets on the tour, so there may be a lesson for us all there. It doesn't matter what it looks like as long as the ball ends up in the right place.

Another time, playing for Middlesex, Edmonds started bowling a mixture of waist-high full tosses and balls that pitched four times before unleashing a fast leg-cutter, *a la* Dennis Lillee in his heyday, which ripped out the off peg of a startled batsman.

At least Edmonds came back from his attack of the jitters. Poor old Keith Medlycott had to quit at the age of 26 when he got the yips and Gavin Hamilton asked to be taken off when he bowled nine no-balls.

In a one-final at Lord's, Scott Boswell threw down nine wides in two overs playing for Leicestershire against Somerset and must have hoped the ground would open and swallow him up. The poor bloke was having every bowler's worst nightmare in front of a full house at Lord's and with millions of people watching on TV. Every bowler who saw that would have thought "there but for the grace of God go I."

I lost my run-up a few times but thankfully it was nothing permanent and I managed to get through my career without too many attacks of the jitters. The thought of faking a bout of the yips when Adam Gilchrist is at the other end butchering the bowling never occurred to me. Honest.

Yorker

A yorker is a ball that pitches right up in the blockhole and is the option of choice for any bowler trying to get rid of a tailender cheaply or bowling at the death of a one-day game. Among current players, Goughie and Waqar Younis are the masters and generally I didn't last long when the ball was spearing in at my stumps.

It also forms part of the oldest three-card trick in the book practised by fast bowlers and mastered, like every other aspect of bowling, by the late Malcolm Marshall. Our careers overlapped but thankfully when the West Indies toured in 1988 they did not play Middlesex. We had a game against the Sri Lankans, which was much safer.

Marshall was one of the most fearsome bowlers ever to play the game and would be a good bet to take the new ball for an Earth XI in a match against Mars. He had this particular trick worked out to the last detail.

He would see a batsman who was a bit nervy against the short stuff and, after giving them a bit of a working over, would work out if they fancied the hook or not.

He would make a great show of altering his field, putting a couple of men back on the fence for the shot and so on so that the poor batsman was convinced he was due for a spot of leather smelling.

His first movement would be back in anticipation of another snorter but Marshall would bowl a yorker instead and stumps would fly everywhere. It almost makes me want to take up fast bowling again.

Zimbabwe

Zimbabwe was front and back page news before the World Cup in South Africa when the ICC refused to move games to South Africa and England then refused to play their games there.

In the good old tradition of cricket administration the whole thing was a complete farce. England said they did not want to go there because of the safety of the players and Robert Mugabe's way of ruling a country, then started squabbling about money and points. The ICC should not have scheduled the games there in the first place.

I will go anywhere in the world to have a game of cricket as long as I am not going to get my head blown off by a sniper when I am at mid-on and I don't have to tread over dead bodies getting to the ground. So on those grounds England should have said, "No thank-you very much, we're not going and you can stick your four points up your arse as well." All the appealing for the points and the row over money made the ECB look terrible and the ICC even worse for staging games in a war zone.

The fact that England were the first major nation due to play a game in Zimbabwe did them no favours either, and the other countries just sat around watching the ECB make fools of themselves, lock their players in the crapper and let Nasser take the rap as they sipped their gin and tonics. Ditto the ICC.

By the time the Aussies came to play there it was pretty obvious that the players and officials would be safe and Mugabe would not dare to use the games for political purposes.

Wisden had it absolutely spot-on when they said that Malcolm Speed and his cronies on the ICC had "shamed the game" by not moving the games from Zimbabwe.

The whole thing rightly took attention away from the cricket for a while, but now the World Cup has finished how much difference has it made?

Zone

Batsmen say that they are in the zone when they have tunnel vision and can block everything out except the flight of the ball. I tried everything in my playing days to get into this trance-like state — I even chanted once as I walked to the wicket — but the only way I could go into a trance was by having a few sherbets. Not really the done thing if you are going out to bat.

Zooter

One of Warnie's biggest strengths is his bare-faced cheek. When he came up with the zooter, to add to his armoury of leggie, googly, slider, toppie, flipper and the rest I thought he had really flipped.

According to the great one, the zooter comes out of the front of the hand and goes straight on — like a million club spinners do for six balls an over every week.

But Warnie turns on the charm in front of the cameras and the batsmen all over the world are turned into dribbling wrecks because they are going to face the Zooter — the ball that goes straight on.

Richie Benaud reckons he was taught to bowl the zooter using an apple but as soon as Warnie starts to talk it up then the ball is the most dangerous thing ever since to man.

Still good luck to him. Bowlers need all the help they can get and if he manages to plant a bit of doubt in some batsmen's minds by talking complete cobblers then it will have been worth it.